He's Working Miracles

DARING TO ASK GOD FOR THE IMPOSSIBLE

Dana Rongione

He's Still Working Miracles:

DARING TO ASK GOD FOR THE IMPOSSIBLE

All Scripture notations are taken from The Holy Bible, KJV.

Copyright © 2016 Dana Rongione

2

How would you like to receive free devotions in your inbox four days a week?

No fees. No catch.
No obligations.

Sign up today at DanaRongione.com.

HE'S STILL WORKING MIRACLES

TABLE OF CONTENTS

HE'S STILL WORKING MIRACLES

INTRODUCTION

*"Miracles are a retelling in small letters of the very
same story which is written across the whole
world in letters too large for some of us to see."*
C.S. Lewis

Have you ever read Lewis Carroll's book, *Alice
in Wonderland*? It's quite a tale and solid evidence of a
vivid imagination gone wild.   But, ironically, it also
contains a valuable lesson for the doubting Christian.
Take a look at this dialogue between Alice and the
Queen of Hearts:

*"There's no use trying," [Alice] said, "one can't
believe impossible things."*

*"I daresay you haven't had much practice," said
the Queen. "When I was your age, I always did it for
half-an-hour a day. Why, sometimes I've believed as
many as six impossible things before breakfast."*

*For you see, so many out-of-the-way things had
happened lately that Alice had begun to think that very
few things were really impossible.*

When did believing in the impossible become so
difficult?   When we were younger, didn't we accept that
Santa Claus could enter our homes through the chimney
and leave presents for boys and girls all around the
world in a single night? Did we struggle to fathom what
desire the tooth fairy could have for our discarded
molars? Was it a stretch of the imagination to believe in
dragons or magic or aliens from another planet?   No.
Back then, believing was easy. It was safe. But oh, how

things have changed. When we were young, we had no perception of the word "impossible." Now it seems to permeate every fiber of our being.

I'm going to get out of this dead-end job and make a real life for myself? Impossible!

One day I'll meet someone who will treat me with the respect I deserve and love me without reservation. Impossible!

I will get out of debt and finally get my finances under control. Impossible!

The doctor's report isn't good, but there's still hope for healing, right? Impossible!

Everywhere we turn, we see impossible people, impossible situations, and impossible deadlines. We're tired and weary, and unlike Alice, we're beginning to wonder whatever happened to the God of possibilities.

When life gets us down, it's easy to forget that the same God who worked miracles back in the Bible days is still working miracles today. It is my hope and prayer that this book will serve as a reminder that we serve a God who never changes, and He won't do any less for His children today than He did for His children back then. He's still working miracles, and He has some in store for you!

How can I speak so confidently? How can I be sure that God still works miracles today? I'm certain because I'm married to one of those miracles.

In August of 1995, my husband (whom I had not yet met) was traveling from his home in south Florida to Greenville, SC, where he was scheduled to attend college. After having stayed up too late the night before, Jason dozed off at the wheel somewhere in Georgia. His

8

car collided head-on with a large dump truck. The truck driver was unharmed, and much to the amazement of all, Jason walked away with only a few scratches and a couple of pieces of glass embedded in his face and arm. His car did not fair so well.

The first night of college, everyone was talking about the guy who had been involved in such a terrible accident and lived to tell the tale. He was a walking, talking miracle. I was thrilled for him and his family. Even though I knew very little about him at the time, I was relieved that God had seen fit to spare his life to further use him for His service. I had no idea that I was part of that plan. What I did know, however, was that God had indeed worked a miracle. There was simply no doubt about it!

Now, I want to help you believe again. By exploring some of the miracles of the New Testament, I hope to show you how to identify miracles in your own life and how to apply the principles of the New Testament miracles to your current circumstances. It is my prayer that the variety of true stories will encourage and inspire you to ask God for the impossible.

If you're struggling to pay your bills and constantly find yourself with more month than money, take comfort in the section entitled "Miracles of Provision." If you're suffering from sickness—whether physical or emotional—turn to the section on "Miracles of Healing." Feeling unloved, forsaken or ineffective? You might enjoy taking a glance at the "Miracles of Love." Each chapter provides an in-depth look at a specific miracle and offers spiritual insight that you can apply to your everyday life and current situation.

You may no longer believe in Santa Claus or the Easter bunny, but I beg you, don't stop believing in God. He's still working miracles, and He excels in doing the impossible!

"A miracle is when the whole is greater than the sum of its parts. A miracle is when one plus one equals a thousand."
Frederick Buechner, The Alphabet of Grace

Section One:
Miracles
of
Provision

HE'S STILL WORKING MIRACLES

Chapter One:

MORE MOUTHS THAN MONEY

After these things Jesus went over the sea of Galilee, which is the sea of Tiberias. And a great multitude followed him, because they saw his miracles which he did on them that were diseased. And Jesus went up into a mountain, and there he sat with his disciples. And the passover, a feast of the Jews, was nigh. When Jesus then lifted up his eyes, and saw a great company come unto him, he saith unto Philip, Whence shall we buy bread, that these may eat? And this he said to prove him: for he himself knew what he would do. Philip answered him, Two hundred pennyworth of bread is not sufficient for them, that every one of them may take a little. One of his disciples, Andrew, Simon Peter's brother, saith unto him, There is a lad here, which hath five barley loaves, and two small fishes: but what are they among so many? And Jesus said, Make the men sit down. Now there was much grass in the place. So the men sat down, in number about five thousand. And Jesus took the loaves; and when he had given thanks, he distributed to the disciples, and the disciples to them that were set down; and likewise of the fishes as much as they would. When they were filled, he said unto his disciples, Gather up the fragments that remain, that nothing be lost. Therefore they gathered them together, and filled twelve baskets with the fragments of the five barley loaves, which remained over and above unto them that had eaten. Then those men, when they had seen the miracle that

13

Jesus did, said, This is of a truth that prophet that should come into the world. - John 6:1-14

Who doesn't love a good picnic? In the twenty years I've known my husband, Jason, we've been on quite a few remarkable picnics. Some of them, I must say, were remarkable for all the wrong reasons. I don't know what it is, but we have a tendency to pick the days with the worst weather conditions for our picnics. Wait, that's not entirely true. At the point we decided to picnic, the weather forecast was fine. It wasn't until we were actually on the picnic that the weather turned nasty.

Our first picnic took place on a rather blustery day. It was cold. Very cold! After that, there was the picnic in the torrential downpour that quickly became a flood. Oh, and perhaps the best of all was on my nineteenth birthday. Jason took me to a lovely little spot in Georgia to propose to me. The romantic little picnic he had so carefully planned only had one hitch—it was snowing! Thankfully, he was driving an SUV at the time. We laid the back seats down, spread out the picnic blanket and partook of our feast while watching out the back window as the snow fell peacefully over the mountains.

We've had some mild picnics too, but to be honest, they are nowhere near as memorable as the ones where we've gone up against the weather and the weather won. No, those picnics are forever etched in my memory. Eventful. Exciting. Exhilarating. Still, they don't compare to the rather large picnic that took place on a hillside in Galilee so many years ago. You could say that inclement weather impacted that picnic as well. While the Bible says nothing about rain clouds, it speaks volumes of the watered-down faith of the disciples. We'd like to think heavenly breezes were blowing, but it was more like gusts of complaints and excuses. As for snow, well, there were flakes on the hillside for sure, and I'm not talking about flurries. According to the dictionary, a flake is "an unreliable person; someone who agrees to do something, but never follows through." That definition seems to fit the misfit crew we find at this momentous picnic. You know, foul-weather friends (yes, pun intended). But we'll get to that soon enough. For now, let's set the scene.

RAINED-OUT REST TIME

Our story begins with delighted disciples, a discouraged Savior, and a determined crowd. Jesus had just received the news that his friend and cousin, John the Baptist, had been beheaded by King Herod. In the midst of his suffering, the disciples arrived from the mission trip on which Jesus had sent them. They were excited and filled with stories of how they had healed the sick and performed other miracles. I imagine the twelve standing in a circle and comparing their tales.

"Guys, you'll never believe this, but I was preaching to this group of people, and a blind man stepped forward and asked to be healed. All I had to do was touch him, and he could see. Isn't that amazing?"

"Yeah, well, I healed a lame man. Yup, the man had never walked a day in his life. I walked right over to him, told him to get up and walk, and he did. He didn't even limp! He walked as sure and steady as if he'd been walking his entire life."

"I healed four lepers."

"Man, that's nothing! You should have seen what I did."

"This performing of miracles is pretty cool stuff. I wonder if we'll get to do it some more."

With a quiet voice, Jesus interrupted their celebration. "Let's go find a quiet place to rest."

No one could blame Jesus for His desire to have some time to Himself. After all, He had spent day after day teaching and healing. His body was tired. His heart was broken by the news He had just received. While we know Jesus was one hundred percent God, we also know that He was one hundred percent man. That means He was subject to the same weariness of the flesh that we are, and that weariness was growing by the hour. Rest sounded like the perfect remedy. Unfortunately, the crowd of people following on His heels had plans of their own.

Hoping to dissuade the growing throng from following them, Jesus and the disciples took a quick boat trip across the sea. Before they could step out onto the shore, the crowd was standing before them. The disciples groaned in disappointment, but Jesus saw the people and had compassion on them. Without hesitation, He led them to the hillside and began teaching them and healing their sick. What an excellent reminder to us that the Lord is never too busy to offer us aid. He is willing to set aside His own comfort and growing needs to be a Shepherd to His sheep. (Mark 6:34)

Everyone was so enthralled with Jesus' teaching that they lost track of time. Seconds turned to minutes and minutes to hours. As the sun began to set, the rumble of stomachs could be heard throughout the crowd. I imagine, though, that the people were willing to endure their hunger just so that they could hear more of what Jesus had to say. How sad that we don't have the same mentality today. I know of people who will get up and walk out of a church service at 12:00 on the dot whether the preacher is finished or not. I call them "clock watchers." Unfortunately, their behavior leads me to believe that they are much more concerned with physical food than with spiritual food.

A bit like the disciples at this point.

THE THUNDER OF COMPLAINTS

Mark 6:35-36 tells us, *And when the day was now far spent, his disciples came unto him, and said, This is a desert place, and now the time is far passed: Send them away, that they may go into the country round about, and into the villages, and buy themselves bread: for they have nothing to eat.* We have to wonder if the disciples were really concerned about the people at this point or if they were concerned about themselves. Did they want Jesus to send the crowd away because the people were hungry or because they were hungry themselves? It just sounds nicer and more spiritual to phrase it the way they did, doesn't it?

I have to admit that I'm guilty of doing the same thing from time to time. Don't get me wrong. I love fellowship as much as the next person. But I also love the comfort of my home and my pajamas and my food. So I have been known, on occasion, to offer up the excuse, "Well, we need to be going. Jason has to go to work early tomorrow" to escape the fellowshippers who just don't know when to stop fellowshipping. Was it true that Jason had to go to work early? Absolutely. Was that my real reason for wanting to depart then? Not usually. Typically, it's more along the lines that I'm tired or hungry or simply wanting to go home. But if I were to say that, it would make me sound bad, like I didn't enjoy their fellowship or something. So, I sink to the level of the disciples and cast the blame elsewhere.

Fortunately, Jesus didn't fall for it. In fact, I imagine He had a quirky little smile on His face when He turned back to the disciples and said, "Well, if they're hungry, feed them!" It sounds like a logical conclusion, but there were a few snags in the plan. First off, the disciples didn't have any food. Second, they didn't have enough money to buy food for a crowd that size.

I can hear their murmurs even now.

"He wants us to feed all these people?"

"Maybe He's been out in the sun too long."

"Feed them? With what?"

Ah, now there's a familiar question. With what? I ask that question nearly every time I sit down to pay the bills. It's the same question that echoes in my mind when I face a daunting task or trying day. Pay the bills? With what money? Complete the task? With what skill? Make it through the day? With what strength? With what? How do we turn nothing into something? By going to the One who excels in doing just that. After all, He spoke this world into existence. Don't we think it's possible He can take care of our petty needs?

Several years ago, a friend of mine was contemplating signing her three children up for a home-school co-op. She had heard so much about this particular group, and after looking into it further, she was convinced that it was perfect for her children. The only problem was that it was going to cost around $1,500. She was a stay-at-home mom, and her husband worked for a landscaping company. Fifteen hundred dollars was a lot of money.

But instead of growing discouraged, my friend prayed. She asked the Lord to provide a way for them to make this work if it was truly in His will. A few days later, she was cleaning out her closet and "happened" to come across a box that was full of graduation cards. After glancing at the first card, my friend made an amazing discovery: the card had money in it. Opening the next card, she found that it, too, had money. Evidently, my dear, sweet friend had forgotten to take the money out of these cards before storing them away in her closet. After she had gone through the entire box, she held $1,400 in her hands. Who forgets about $1,400? I'm not even sure I've ever had that much money to forget about!

My friend had her answer, and the next day, she signed her children up for co-op, a group that they are still a part of today. Not only did God provide that first year's tuition, but He's provided for every year since then. If you had asked my friend how she thought God was going to provide the money, I guarantee you that finding money in a box of old graduation cards wouldn't have even made the list. God works outside the realm of our logic and even our imagination. We ask, "With what?" and all the while God is saying, "Don't worry. I've got it taken care of. Trust me." Unfortunately, we are often too deafened by our doubts to hear Him, much like the disciples.

TESTING IN THE TEMPEST

When Jesus then lifted up his eyes, and saw a great company come unto him, he saith unto Philip, Whence shall we buy bread, that these may eat? And this he said to prove him: for he himself knew what he would do. (John 6:5-6)

Do you remember the ear-piercing tests they used to do for the emergency broadcast system? I can remember, as a child, having my favorite music or television program interrupted with these words: "This is a test of the emergency broadcast system. This is only a test." Immediately following was a long beep that seemed to get longer every time I heard it. Remember now? Well, insert that right here into the story. Jesus asked the disciples about feeding the crowd, but notice what verse six says. His question was a test. Jesus already knew what He was going to do. His plan was already in place. He didn't need the disciples' advice, suggestions, or aid. He had everything under control. But did the disciples realize that?

Philip was the first to take the test. Jesus wanted to know how much money they had, and Philip answered, "Not enough." Wrong answer! Jesus wasn't asking what they *didn't* have. He was asking what they *did* have. It's too bad Philip suffered from the same limited eyesight that often leaves us feeling down and depressed. We're so focused on the things we want and

21

don't have that we neglect to see all the things we do have.

We don't have a fancy house, so we fail to be thankful for the roof over our heads.

We don't have a lot of money in the bank, so we fail to notice how God meets our needs despite our lack of funds.

We don't have a good-paying job, so we take for granted the fact that we have a good job that is well-suited to our talents and personalities.

God asks us, "What do you have, child?"

And we answer, "Not enough."

And we fail the test. Just like Philip.

Thankfully, we serve a good God who can turn our biggest failures into life-altering lessons. Philip illustrated the first step we need to take in surrendering our lives to God. He admitted that he couldn't solve the problem. He didn't have what it takes. By pointing out that they didn't have enough money, Jesus was saying, "You don't have the means to solve this problem yourself." Likewise, sometimes the Lord has to point out our deficiencies to remind us that we can't remedy the situation by ourselves. We don't have the strength. We don't have the power. We don't have the means. But He does!

That point being established, Jesus moved on to the next disciple. Andrew, determined to pass this test, went out into the crowd to ascertain what food could be gathered. He returned to Jesus, not only with some food but with an answer to Jesus' original question of "What do we have?" He plopped down a rusty lunch pail and informed Jesus, "There's a lad here who's offered his lunch. There are five loaves and two fish in there. . ." If Andrew had stopped there, he may have passed the test.

But he didn't.

Instead, he continued on, "But that won't be enough."

But. . . That is one dangerous word, and it can wreak havoc in our lives. Unfortunately, it's used too frequently in the nasty now and now. It looks innocent enough, doesn't it? Just a common little conjunction. What harm could it possibly do? Read the following examples and see if you can figure it out:

I know smoking is bad for me, *but* it makes me feel better, at least temporarily.

I know I shouldn't eat this piece of chocolate cake, *but* I've had a hard day.

I know this isn't the best decision, *but* I'm tired of trying to figure it out.

I know God's promises are true, *but* I don't see Him working in this situation.

I know I have a loving wife at home, *but* my secretary really understands me.

I know I should read my Bible more, *but* I just don't have the time.

I know that Jesus can do the impossible, *but* there simply isn't enough here for Him to work with.

Whether the situation is big or small, the word "but" seems to make our excuses permissible. We know what's right, but we still do what's wrong. And for some reason, we act like it's okay because we do know better. How messed up is that? It's not better; it's worse. The Bible says so in James 4:17, *Therefore to him that knoweth to do good, and doeth it not, to him it is sin.* It doesn't get any clearer. If we know to do right, and we don't do it, we're sinning against God. No "ifs," "ands," and especially no "buts."

By stating that they didn't have enough, Andrew made his answer the same as Philip's. Sure, he was looking to what they did have rather than what they didn't, but he was still missing a big piece of the puzzle. They all were. In fact, they all appeared to be suffering from a severe case of spiritual amnesia. They'd been traveling with Jesus for how long now? They'd seen Him work how many miracles? And if that weren't enough, allow me to take you on a short trip down memory lane and show you what went on during the days preceding this perilous predicament.

SHOWERS OF BLESSING

Then he called his twelve disciples together, and gave them power and authority over all devils, and to cure diseases. And he sent them to preach the kingdom of God, and to heal the sick. And he said unto them, Take nothing for your journey, neither staves, nor scrip, neither bread, neither money; neither have two coats apiece. And whatsoever house ye enter into, there abide, and thence depart. And whosoever will not receive you, when ye go out of that city, shake off the very dust from your feet for a testimony against them. And they departed, and went through the towns, preaching the gospel, and healing every where. (Luke 9:1-6)

I don't know about you, but when I go on a trip, I tend to over-pack. I'm always afraid I might need this or

24

that, so I'd rather pack it and not need it than need it and not have it. Unfortunately, the size of my pack or suitcase tends to grow the more I contemplate what I "might" need. Will it be hot or cold? Will it be wet or dry? Will it be dressy or casual? Decisions. Decisions.

I guess you could say that Jesus made it easy for the disciples to pack. They weren't allowed to take anything with them. Nothing! No staff for protection from wild animals. No food. No money. Not even an extra coat or a change of shoes. He basically sent them out with the clothes on their backs—oh, and the power of God!

And look at what they accomplished. *And they went out, and preached that men should repent. And they cast out many devils, and anointed with oil many that were sick, and healed them. (Mark 6:12-13)* It seems to me that, even though they weren't allowed any provisions, they had everything they needed and then some. Not in any of the four gospels do we see a record of any of the disciples going hungry or being in any form of need during this time. In fact, during the Last Supper in Luke, Jesus asked, "When I sent you without purse, and scrip, and shoes, lacked ye any thing?" And the disciples answer, "Nothing." Though they took nothing with them, all their needs were met. Beyond that, they were able to perform miracles. Casting out devils and healing the sick were no simple feats. Yet, the disciples didn't bat an eye at their abilities.

At least, not until this point in the story, when their bodies were tired, and their faith was weak. Now, these wonder-working wanderers were stumped. They saw the problem, but for the life of them, they couldn't see the solution. Even though He was standing right beside them. I like the way Max Lucado puts it: *If faith is a candle, those fellows were in the dark.* Despite all they had seen in the past, they simply couldn't figure out what to do.

Fortunately, there was one (other than Christ) who knew what to do, and he was probably one of the youngest people in the crowd. He was certainly younger than any of the disciples. Though the Bible doesn't tell us much about the lad who offered his lunch to Jesus, I truly believe he exhibited a practice that many of us struggle with day after day.

He gave what he had to Jesus and left the results up to Him.

So often we're deceived by the notion that we can take care of our own problems or that we can take care of them better than God can. We plot and scheme, struggle and strive, and in the end, we've only succeeded in making a big mess. Then, we sit in our pit of despair and wonder how to get out of the worsened situation. If only we would learn to take it to Jesus and leave it there.

Unlike the lad who came in faith, we come with our adult intelligence. When we can't see God's plan or figure out how things are going to work, we doubt God's ability to handle the situation. After analyzing the situation further, we determine that it would be in our best interest to figure it out for ourselves. And all faith is abandoned.

Which is why the twelve disciples were standing around scratching their heads and trying to figure out how to solve their current dilemma. Philip was counting coins. Andrew was crunching numbers. James was searching his pockets. Judas, no doubt, was hoarding what little money they did have. Not one of them looked to Jesus. Not one of them thought to offer up a prayer. Sadly, when we don't look up, we tend to give up. Just as the twelve were about to do when Jesus interrupted their thoughts. "Divide the people into groups on the hillside, and tell them we're getting ready to eat."

HEAVENLY BREEZES

It was an odd request, to say the least. As far as the disciples knew, there still wasn't enough food to feed all those people. Even if there was, why divide the people into groups? Why not just tell everybody to sit down?

It could be that through this one simple act, Jesus was reminding us that He does all things "decently and in order."[1]

Or it could be that grouping the people together made it easier to count them. Think about it, which sounds more impressive to you: Jesus fed a lot of people or Jesus fed 5,000 men plus women and children? There's really no way to know why Jesus made this request, but one thing we can be fairly sure of is that the disciples didn't ask. They just did it. Oh, that we could learn to do the same! To get it through our heads that we don't have to understand the hows and whys; we just need to obey.

At this point, Jesus did what the disciples had failed to do. He lifted His head towards Heaven and offered a blessing for the food. Though the meal was meager, Jesus gave thanks. He didn't complain about the lack or ask for more. He merely gave gratitude for what was given. And then He moved on to the next phase of His plan.

Jesus began breaking the bread and fish into little pieces. Twelve baskets were brought forth (one for each disciple), and Jesus filled each basket with food. At this point in the story, the Bible gives us a little room for speculation. We know that the disciples took the food to the people and that everyone ate until they were satisfied. What we're left to imagine is the process itself.

It's possible that the baskets of food became like the widow's barrel in the story of Elijah.[2]

It's reasonable to assume that every time one of the disciples reached into the basket, there was enough food for the person he was serving. Then as he moved on to the next person, there was enough for one serving again. In other words, they never reached the bottom of the basket.

It's also possible that the baskets remained full even though the food was constantly being passed out to the people. But, as a former kindergarten teacher of nine years, I like to stretch my imagination, so I choose to believe that it happened something like this:

John took his basket, marveling at the amount of food provided from such a small lunch yet still doubting that there was enough to feed all the people. He wandered over to the first group and passed out portions of the meal. As he scraped the bottom of the basket to feed the last of that group, he shook his head. *I knew there wasn't enough. Maybe I shouldn't have given them so much. I'll go ask Jesus what He wants me to do now.*

With his head bowed low, he approached Jesus. "There isn't enough," he muttered. "What should we do now?" Jesus remained silent, so John looked up to find Jesus smiling—not so much a happy smile, but more an amused one. In confusion, John tried to hand his empty basket to Jesus but was shocked to discover that it's full once again. He looked to Jesus whose only response was a smile and a quick flick of His wrist to shoo John back to work.

Time and time again, each disciple emptied his basket and returned to Jesus only to find it full once again. By constantly running out of food and having to return to Christ, the disciples were learning an important lesson: when in need, go to Jesus. He is the Source. Without Him, we can do nothing. When you've hit rock bottom, you know where to turn. He'll always be waiting to give you what you need.

HERE COMES THE DOWNPOUR

After the people had their fill, Jesus told the disciples to gather up all the leftovers. Leftovers? There wasn't enough to begin with, yet when the disciples finished their rounds, they found themselves holding twelve baskets full of food. Do you realize that they ended up with more food than they started with? And could it be a coincidence that there was one basket for each of the twelve disciples? I don't believe in coincidences.

No, I believe in this simple act, Jesus was saying, "Not only have I provided for today's need, but I've done far beyond. You had a meal tonight, and now you each have meals for tomorrow as well."

The Bible tells us that God does *exceeding abundantly more than we ask or think.*[3]

He is not just the God of enough; He's the God of more than enough. Not only can He meet our current needs, but He can provide for the future as well. Just as with the disciples, God has our well-being in mind. He knows what we need, and He knows what is best for us. He has a plan for our lives. Could it be that He's simply waiting for us to give Him what we have so that He can multiply it into what we need?

Chapter Two:

THE GREAT ESCAPE

Now about that time Herod the king stretched forth his hands to vex certain of the church. And he killed James the brother of John with the sword. And because he saw it pleased the Jews, he proceeded further to take Peter also. (Then were the days of unleavened bread.) And when he had apprehended him, he put him in prison, and delivered him to four quaternions of soldiers to keep him; intending after Easter to bring him forth to the people. Peter therefore was kept in prison: but prayer was made without ceasing of the church unto God for him. And when Herod would have brought him forth, the same night Peter was sleeping between two soldiers, bound with two chains: and the keepers before the door kept the prison. And, behold, the angel of the Lord came upon him, and a light shined in the prison: and he smote Peter on the side, and raised him up, saying, Arise up quickly. And his chains fell off from his hands. And the angel said unto him, Gird thyself, and bind on thy sandals. And so he did. And he saith unto him, Cast thy garment about thee, and follow me. And he went out, and followed him; and wist not that it was true which was done by the angel; but thought he saw a vision. When they were past the first and the second ward, they came unto the iron gate that leadeth unto the city; which opened to them of his own accord: and they went out, and passed on through one street; and forthwith the angel departed from him. And when Peter was come to

31

himself, he said, Now I know of a surety, that the LORD hath sent his angel, and hath delivered me out of the hand of Herod, and from all the expectation of the people of the Jews. And when he had considered the thing, he came to the house of Mary the mother of John, whose surname was Mark; where many were gathered together praying. And as Peter knocked at the door of the gate, a damsel came to hearken, named Rhoda. And when she knew Peter's voice, she opened not the gate for gladness, but ran in, and told how Peter stood before the gate. And they said unto her, Thou art mad. But she constantly affirmed that it was even so. Then said they, It is his angel. But Peter continued knocking: and when they had opened the door, and saw him, they were astonished. But he, beckoning unto them with the hand to hold their peace, declared unto them how the Lord had brought him out of the prison. And he said, Go shew these things unto James, and to the brethren. And he departed, and went into another place. - Acts 12:1-17

A couple of nights ago, a vicious storm hit our area. The rain fell in sheets. The lightning shone so brightly it was like daytime. The wind howled, and the thunder rattled the house like an earthquake. It was some of the strangest thunder I had ever heard. It began as a rumble, then turned into a roll. Then, in the midst of the roll, it boomed and shook the house violently. When the shaking ceased, the roll of the thunder continued on for what seemed like minutes. I lay awake for over an hour, listening to the storm around me and marveling at the fact that my husband and two dogs were sleeping soundly. The next morning, when I asked Jason about the storm, his reply was, "It stormed last night?" Not only had he slept through it, but he was also unaware that the storm had even occurred. I always knew he was a sound sleeper, but that's simply ridiculous!

On the night before his execution, do we see Peter in a panic? Do we see him crying to the Lord as he did on the storm-tossed sea, "Don't you care that I'm about to die?" No, that's not the picture the Bible gives us. Instead, we find Peter asleep, head resting on the shoulder of one of the guards. His slumber leads us to believe that perhaps he had finally learned a few lessons from the Master. This was not the doubting, denying Peter. This was the changed Peter. The bold Peter. The believing Peter. This was Peter at peace with his lot in life. Resting in the knowledge that God is in control of all things, Peter was able to sleep through his storm just as Jesus had slept through the storm on the Sea of Galilee. Fear didn't plague his mind. Worry didn't hinder his dreams. In fact, it took an angel to stir him.

WAKEY, WAKEY

In the middle of the night, a great light filled the prison. That, alone, would have awakened me, but not Peter. No, he slept on. A mighty angel appeared at Peter's side, but still, Peter took no notice. Again, there's something about a presence nearby that wakes me out of the deepest slumber. I can be dead to the world, but suddenly a sense of panic assails me. Even with my eyes closed, I can tell someone is near, perhaps even looking at me. Typically, when I open one eye to discover the source of my discomfort, I find my 90-pound dog, Mitch, wedged between Jason and me, his eyes staring down at me as if to say, "Is it time for breakfast?" I doubt, however, that even Mitch could have snapped Peter out of his zombie-like state.

The angel, eager to be about his business, poked Peter. Nothing. Grabbing Peter's shoulder and giving him a gentle shake, he whispered, "Peter, wake up." Peter blinked a time or two then rubbed his face trying to wipe the sleep from his eyes. "Come on," the angel said, "get up now." As the chains fell away from Peter's wrists, he clumsily pulled himself to his feet. "Put your shoes and coat on," the angel reminded the muddle-headed Peter.

I'm sorry, but that part of the story makes me laugh out loud. The entire scene is reminiscent of the years I spent teaching kindergarten. After lunch, we would have a fifteen-minute quiet time where I would turn out the lights and turn on some soft music so the students could lay their heads on their desks and rest. It was a good chance to allow their food to settle and for each of them to regain some energy for the rest of the day's lessons. Immediately following this rest time was a short recess. Inevitably, at least one child (though usually more than that) would fall asleep during the brief rest time. Rousing the children was never a dull affair, especially if more than one had fallen asleep. After getting the first one woke up, I would move on to the second. By the time that one was roused, the first one had often fallen back asleep. Once everyone was awake, the drama continued. "Okay, you need to put your coat on," I would say. The student would look at me bleary-eyed. "Go get your coat from your cubby," I'd prod. Still, they'd stare as if I were speaking a foreign language. To speed up the process, I'd grab the coat and hand it to the child. They would hold it but nothing more. For some, it would take me holding the coat and walking them through the process. "Put your arm in the sleeve. No, not that one. The other arm. Yes, that's right. Okay, now put this arm in this sleeve. That's good. Okay, let's zip it up. No, the zipper is in the front. That means you need to look at me so I can zip it up for you." Any of you who have ever dealt with a sleepy child know exactly what I'm talking about. What's so funny to me is that here we have an angel talking to a grown man as if he were nothing more than a child. "Put your shoes on. Yes, that's right. No, that one goes on the other foot. Okay, good. Now, let's put your coat on." It strikes me as hilarious!

Once Peter was ready, the angel took him by the hand and led him through the prison. Keep in mind, the place was crawling with soldiers. In fact, we know that there were soldiers on either side of Peter as he slept. There were soldiers within and soldiers without. Nevertheless, the angel and Peter strolled through the fortress, past guard after guard who were either asleep or completely unaware of the escapee. One wonders if Peter and his angel were invisible for this little midnight outing or if maybe God had put blinders over the eyes of the guards. Whatever the case, their escape was unimpeded. And Peter, bless his heart, still thought he was dreaming.

OPEN SESAME

As they arrived at the outer gate, it swung open of its own accord. At least, that's what I always thought the Bible said. I'm amazed at how such little, seemingly insignificant words can have such a powerful impact on a particular verse. If you look very carefully, you'll notice that the Bible actually says the gate swung open of "his" own accord. Whose own accord? The angel's? Peter's? I doubt it since Peter still thought he was having a dream. I like to think it was God's accord. After all, this was his rescue mission. That being said, I believe much can be gleaned from that open gate.

In our Christian walk, we will come to many doors. Some are open; some are shut. When God places an open door in our lives, it seems pretty obvious what He would have us to do. But I caution you, an open door does not always indicate God's will. For example, Jason recently heard of a job opening that sounded like the answer to the prayers we had been praying for months. He had been looking for a new opportunity with more stable hours and a better paycheck. We prayed. The door opened. Yet neither of us had peace about it. Before making a rash decision, we continued to pray for God's clear direction. In fact, I remember my prayer like it was just yesterday. It went like this: "Lord, you know the situation we're in, and you know our need. A door has opened before us, but neither of us feels your peace. Lord, please show us what to do. If You want us to take this job, we will. If you want us to wait where we are so that You can give us something better down the road, we're willing to do that too. We just need to know, Lord. Please make it clear." Oh boy, did he!

That night, as Jason and I sat down to have our devotions, we pulled out our new devotional book, Oswald Chambers' *My Utmost for His Highest,* and turned to the day's reading. Here's the message that greeted us:

There are times when you can't understand why you cannot do what you want to do. When God brings a time of waiting, and appears to be unresponsive, don't fill it with busyness, just wait. The time of waiting may come to teach you the meaning of sanctification – to be set apart from sin and made holy – or it may come after the process of sanctification has begun to teach you what service means. Never run before God gives you his direction. If you have the slightest doubt, then He is not guiding. Whenever there is doubt – wait.[1]

As if that wasn't clear enough, God's message continued over the next several days. Everything we read, every song we heard, every message that was preached dealt with waiting. Even though the door had been opened and it initially seemed as if God was answering our prayers concerning a new job, God's leading told us differently. For the time being, God wanted us to wait. So we stood in the hallway and watched as the door slammed shut.

If you find yourself facing an open door, you need to ask yourself, "Is this the will of God?" If you don't have absolute peace that it is, don't go through the door. Just wait. Seek God's face. Ask Him to make His will known to you. He will. In Peter's case, the angel of the Lord personally led him to the open gate, so there was really little need for him to wonder about God's will. If only it were so simple for us, right?

Unfortunately, closed doors aren't any easier to deal with. Often the door leads to something that we long to have or pursue, but for whatever reason, we can't seem to reach it. No matter how much we whine, cry, or pray, the door simply won't budge. In such a case, God may be telling us that He doesn't want us to have that thing. In His loving wisdom, He is instructing us that the things beyond that door are not best for us. On the other hand, God may have every intention of allowing us to walk through that door, but only in His time. The gate didn't open for Peter until God allowed it. God will open the proper doors in our lives when it's the right time. We simply need to be patient and attentive, watching for the open doors and listening to the warnings concerning the closed ones. Jason and I also learned that one the hard way.

For many years, when Jason and I were first married, Jason worked for a production company that did woodworking. It was a decent job, and he was very skilled at the work, but the pay was poor. When combined with my pay as a Christian school teacher, our income was barely enough to survive.

During that time, my dad, brother, and brother-in-law all worked for a company that specialized in computers and programming. Not only did they make good incomes, but they received multiple raises and bonuses throughout the year. For years, Jason and I prayed that Jason could also get a position working for the company. After all, there were family connections, and Jason was very skilled in working with computers. It seemed to be the perfect solution to our financial problems.

But for all the prayers we prayed and the tears we cried, God did not see fit to allow Jason a position in this company. We were confused, disappointed, and frustrated. We could not understand how a loving God would deny such a simple request. That is, until the day the company began laying off employees. My father, brother, and brother-in-law were forced to go to work each day, always wondering if that day would be their last. It was a very stressful time for everyone in the family. Even now, I can remember the moment I understood why God had denied our prayers. We thought we had been asking for a good thing, but God, in his infinite wisdom, knew the future of the company. He lovingly denied our present desire because he knew it was for our best. That's the way God works.

TO MARY'S HOUSE WE GO

After walking through the gate, Peter found himself alone, strolling down the street. He decided to head toward the home of Mary, the mother of John Mark. This was the place where the prayer warriors of the church had gathered. They, no doubt, had been in prayer since Peter's arrest, and they were not going to allow anything to distract them from their efforts. Even the answer to their prayers.

Upon arriving at the house, Peter knocked on the door. A servant girl named Rhoda answered, and recognizing his voice, ran back to the prayer warriors, leaving Peter to stand outside and continue knocking. "It's Peter!" she exclaimed. "He's here. He's at the door!"

Some of the people looked up from their prayers in disgust. "Give me a break. Can't you see we're trying to pray here?"

Undeterred, Rhoda continued, "But it's really him. Peter is free."

No doubt, some of the people grew a little perturbed. "That's quite enough, Rhoda. This is not a laughing matter. Peter really needs our prayers." To appease her, some of the more compassionate souls said, "Perhaps it is just his angel." Some of the more mean-spirited types went so far as to call her crazy. But before she could speak again, another knock was heard.

I would love to have seen Peter's expression at this point. He knocked and knocked and knocked. He knew there were people inside. He could hear them talking, yelling, and praying. He was even pretty sure he had heard his name a few times.

Still, no one came to the door.

I don't know who finally opened the door, but when they did, the house grew quiet. The people sat there, their mouths agape. Some of them were probably thinking, *It's Peter. How in the world did he get here? How did he escape from prison? This just isn't possible.*

40

What they had forgotten is that God specializes in the impossible. The good news for them (and us) is that He doesn't require us to have mountain-sized faith before He works. These people obviously didn't have much faith at all. Sure, they were praying, but we have to wonder if they were truly expecting any results. Hmm, sounds familiar, doesn't it?

How often do we pray for things because we know it's the right thing to do, but in the back of our minds, we know that what we're asking for is impossible? Even when I find I'm able to pray, believing that God can, I find it difficult to pray and believe that God will. Thankfully, Jesus said that if we have faith the size of a mustard seed, we can move mountains. Surely, we can muster up that much faith, right? You would think. But why is it then that, like the early church, we stand gazing in unbelief when the answer to our prayers is right before us? What a patient God we serve to put up with our constant doubt!

EXPLAINING THE UNEXPLAINABLE

Peter held up his hand to silence the commotion that had begun around him. He explained that the Lord saw fit to deliver him from prison and then commanded them to go out and tell others what had happened. In his brief explanation, Peter was able to remind the church that Satan cannot thwart God's plan. God has many ways of accomplishing His will, and while we may not understand those ways, we can rest assured that His will *will* be done.

41

This story of deliverance, for example, is difficult to understand. We see the rescue of Peter, but we also bear witness to the murder of James. Why didn't God rescue them both? Why did God allow James to be murdered? These queries lead us to one of the most commonly asked questions of all time: Why do bad things happen to good people?

I can't answer that question, though not for the reasons you may think. I can't answer it for the sheer reason that the question itself is flawed. The question assumes that there is such a thing as a "good person." But the Bible tells us differently.

For example, Romans 3:10-12 says, *As it is written, There is none righteous, no, not one: There is none that understandeth, there is none that seeketh after God. They are all gone out of the way, they are together become unprofitable; there is none that doeth good, no, not one.*

Additionally, Mark 10:17-18 tells us, *And when he was gone forth into the way, there came one running, and kneeled to him, and asked him, Good Master, what shall I do that I may inherit eternal life? And Jesus said unto him, Why callest thou me good? there is none good but one, that is, God.*

To say one is "good" is a very subjective statement. Good by whose standards? Good compared to whom? We judge goodness by a standard of living. Those who live right and try to serve God, we consider to be "good people." Unfortunately, that is not the standard by which goodness is judged. Christ himself said that only one is good, and that is God. So the question should not be "Why do bad things happen to *good* people?" But rather, "Why do bad things happen to people?"

From there, I can give you an answer, though I doubt it will bring you much comfort. Bad things happen to people so that God may be glorified. Think back to the story where Jesus and His disciples encountered the blind man. The disciples asked Jesus, "Master, who did sin, this man, or his parents, that he was born blind?" Jesus answered them, "Neither hath this man sinned, nor his parents: but that the works of God should be made manifest in him." In other words, nobody did anything wrong. The man wasn't born blind as a punishment. He was born blind so that he could become a tool in the work of the Lord. If the blind man had known that, do you suppose it would have been easier on him? It's hard to say. Being a tool for God is certainly a noble calling, but sometimes it can also be very painful. Just ask Nick Vujicic.

Nick was born without arms or legs. The doctors were baffled by his condition. His parents were rightfully discouraged by his handicap. And Nick, as he grew, became increasingly depressed over his limitations. According to Nick, "As a boy trying to come to terms with my disabilities, I made the mistake of thinking no one else hurt as I did and that my problems were insurmountable. I thought that my lack of limbs was proof that God did not love me and that my life had no purpose. I also felt that I could not share my burdens—even with those who loved and cared about me."[2]

Nick's life was full of struggles and triumphs, sadness and joy, dreams and fears. For many years, Nick struggled to understand why God had made him different. He, too, wrestled with the question of how a perfect God could make such a horrible mistake. There were even times, when the weight of his circumstances seemed overwhelming, that Nick thought of ending it all. Fortunately, Nick was raised to understand that God still had a purpose and plan for his life.

Nick is currently a motivational speaker, evangelist, author, and the director of the nonprofit organization, Life Without Limbs. He travels the world, reaching out to millions of people and sharing his inspirational story. He is a source of hope and encouragement to many who are hurting, and especially to those who suffer from handicaps of their own. Though he still has bad days, as we all do, he no longer questions God's reason for making him the way he is. It took time, but he now clearly sees the path God has laid before him. But don't take my word for it. Let Nick tell you himself.

Being born without arms and legs was not God's way of punishing me. I know that now. I have come to realize that this 'disability' would actually heighten my ability to serve His purpose as a speaker and evangelist. You might be tempted to think that I'm making a huge leap of faith to feel that way, since most people consider my lack of limbs a huge handicap. Instead, God has used my lack of limbs to draw people to me, especially others with disabilities, so I can inspire and encourage them with my messages of faith, hope, and love.[3]

WHAT ARE YOU LOOKING AT?

Unfortunately, the question of why bad things happen to good people is not the only thing that's flawed. Our viewpoint is flawed as well. We read the passage at the beginning of this chapter and assume that James was not delivered, but if we truly think about it, he was. James was delivered from this earthly life into the everlasting life awaiting him in Heaven. He was delivered from a life of pain and turmoil to one of everlasting peace. He was delivered from persecution into a land of rest. I believe if we were to ask James, he would tell us that he was pleased with his deliverance.

Because James was not delivered in the same way Peter was, we wrongfully assume that Peter got off better than James. But the truth is, James made out very well. As my pastor often says, "Don't threaten me with Heaven." James wasn't afraid to die, for he knew what was waiting for him. But more importantly, he knew Who was waiting for him.

We need to come to the realization that God's ways are not our ways and that He doesn't work the same way in every life or every situation. Yes, He is an unchanging God, but that does not mean that He is bound to work within our rules and limitations. He is God. We know that he has a plan for each of us, and my plan may be different from your plan. And that's okay because, no matter what, we can rest assured that God is in control.

We must be careful, however, that our acceptance of God's plan for our lives does not keep us from praying. Many take the attitude of "Well, if God is going to do whatever He wants, then why should I pray?" We should pray, first of all, because it is commanded of us. Secondly, we should pray because our prayers do make a difference. James 5:16 tells us, *The effectual fervent prayer of a righteous man availeth much.* Prayer has the power to change things, but more than that, it has the power to change us. Dr. Charles Stanley says,

As we kneel before God and He pours Himself into us, we in turn give ourselves in devotion to Him. The result is that God places within us a passion for obedience. We want to obey God. Nobody has to prod us. We don't have to hear sermons to make us obey Him. Obedience is now part of our inner beings. We can be tired, weary, and emotionally distraught, but after spending time alone with God, we find that He injects into our bodies energy, power, and strength. God's spiritual dynamics are at work in our inner beings, refreshing and energizing our minds and spirits. There is nothing to match meditation in its impact upon our lives and the lives of others.[4]

Do you ever feel like a prisoner? As Christians, we were once held captive by sin, but thanks to the grace of God, we are freed from that captivity. But does that mean we are no longer bound by anything? I don't know about you, but I often feel like Peter, though my prison has no bars or chains. Rather, I'm held captive by a body that can't seem to keep up with my life goals and ambitions. I'm imprisoned by my finances (or lack thereof). I'm enslaved by the restraints of time. Unlike Peter, however, I find little rest or peace in my jail cell.

When circumstances beyond our control bind us to a life we never expected or a problem we're unable to solve, freedom from our bonds (whatever they may be) always seems to be just out of reach. The prison doors have slammed shut, and we don't have the key. Is God able to deliver us as He did Peter? Not only is He able, He is willing, though we should keep in mind that deliverance may not come in the form in which we are hoping. God will open the prison gates, allowing us to walk boldly into a life of true freedom. According to Warren Wiersbe, "True freedom is doing whatever God wants us to do because that is what is best for us. We find freedom in obedience, true joy in submission."[5]

Perhaps that's why Peter could sleep so soundly in his prison cell. The bars and chains of the prison couldn't deny his true freedom. He was obedient to God, and in that obedience, he found both peace and joy. What about you? Are you longing for the type of peace that will allow you to rest through the fiercest of storms? Do you struggle with finding joy in your life? Could it be that the chains around your wrists are of your own making? Freedom is waiting. You need only to surrender your life to God. We often sing the old hymn, "I Surrender All," but I wonder how many times we're actually paying attention to the promise we're making. Those words hold the key to our spiritual prison, but they must be said in earnest. Nothing short of absolute surrender will bring us true peace. Peter's life was in God's hand, and Peter could rest soundly in that knowledge. Can you?

HE'S STILL WORKING MIRACLES

Section Two:

Miracles

of

Usefulness

HE'S STILL WORKING MIRACLES

Chapter Three:

MARY HAD A LITTLE LAMB

And in the sixth month the angel Gabriel was sent from God unto a city of Galilee, named Nazareth, To a virgin espoused to a man whose name was Joseph, of the house of David; and the virgin's name was Mary. And the angel came in unto her, and said, Hail, thou that art highly favoured, the Lord is with thee: blessed art thou among women. And when she saw him, she was troubled at his saying, and cast in her mind what manner of salutation this should be. And the angel said unto her, Fear not, Mary: for thou hast found favour with God. And, behold, thou shalt conceive in thy womb, and bring forth a son, and shalt call his name JESUS. He shall be great, and shall be called the Son of the Highest: and the Lord God shall give unto him the throne of his father David: And he shall reign over the house of Jacob for ever; and of his kingdom there shall be no end. Then said Mary unto the angel, How shall this be, seeing I know not a man? And the angel answered and said unto her, The Holy Ghost shall come upon thee, and the power of the Highest shall overshadow thee: therefore also that holy thing which shall be born of thee shall be called the Son of God. And, behold, thy cousin Elisabeth, she hath also conceived a son in her old age: and this is the sixth month with her, who was called barren. For with God nothing shall be impossible. And Mary said, Behold the handmaid of the Lord; be it unto me according to thy word. And the angel departed from her. - Luke 1:26-38

From the moment I laid eyes on it, I knew it was something special. As I pulled the book from the shelf, its age became evident. The binding was worn. The cover was scratched and marred. The pages, while in surprisingly good condition, were yellowed with age. Yet the beauty and worth of this volume were unmistakable. I had come across a 1947 version of Leaves of Gold, an anthology of prayers, memorable phrases, and inspirational verse and prose. In my excitement over my good fortune, I neglected to think about the price of such a prize. Yes, I was shopping in one of my favorite thrift stores, but surely something as special as this would be worth far more than I had to give.

After scanning through the pages of my newfound treasure, I looked around at the shelves to see if I could spot a price. I cannot describe to you my elation at discovering that the volume in my hands cost only a dollar. Dollar in hand, I hurried to the checkout counter. As soon as the cashier saw my purchase, she echoed the first word that came to my lips when I saw the book—"Ooh!"

She, too, couldn't help but flip through the pages of the old volume. With a smile, I handed her my dollar, grabbed my book, and walked out the door. As soon as I reached my car, I took my phone out of my purse so that I could take a picture of my treasure and send it to my husband, Jason. I was so excited that I just couldn't wait to share. His texted reply came in quickly and read, "That's nice, but what is Leaves of Gold?" What I had failed to take into consideration was that a mere picture could not describe all that the book contained. To see its true beauty, it was necessary to look beneath the surface.

A lot like Mary, the mother of Jesus.

When people looked at Mary, they didn't see anything special. After all, a young, poor Galilean girl didn't stir much interest. And although the Bible doesn't speak much of Mary's childhood, we can assume that it was far from extraordinary. Like all the other young women, Mary took care of the chores around the house. She sewed, cooked, and drew water from the well. No one knew the future that was awaiting her.

When God looked at Mary, on the other hand, He looked beyond her gender and her poverty. God looked straight into her heart, and from what Gabriel told Mary, God liked what He saw. He saw a heart of trust and a spirit of obedience. He saw a young girl who was willing to do whatever was necessary to please God. He saw a useful vessel, so He used her in a way that could have never been imagined.

A TALE TO BE TREASURED

Picture a young Mary, probably in her early to mid-teens, as she stood before Gabriel. First of all, the shock of seeing an angel had to be overwhelming. Add to this the fact that the angel was showering her with praise. I'm sure Mary was speechless for a little while. But after Gabriel made the announcement of the birth of the Messiah, Mary found that she could no longer hold her tongue. Curiosity won out over caution.

"Let me see if I have this straight," Mary stated. "I'm going to have a child, and this child is going to be the Messiah that we've been waiting for. But how is that possible? I've never had relations with a man."

I imagine Mary's face turned red at this last confession. It's not every day you discuss your virginity with an angel (or anyone else for that matter). Still, Mary was confused and rightly so. She knew the ways of life. She understood the birds and the bees. From her point of view, the thing Gabriel was telling her was impossible.

Have you ever been there? In seemingly impossible situations, I mean. Have you ever found yourself shaking your head and muttering, "There's just no way"? I recall the words from a song that paints the picture so vividly in my mind: "There's a storm on the horizon, and everywhere I turn, it seems as if I've tried that way before."[1]

No way out.

No hope.

No answers.

As strange as it may seem, when I think back over my life and all the many seemingly impossible situations that I have faced, a particular hike with Jason and our dogs comes to my mind. For whatever reason, Jason and I decided to tackle a tough hike in a nearby state park. We knew the hike was rated as extremely strenuous, but we felt that we could handle it. After all, we were in pretty good shape and had been hiking on a regular basis for a while. So, we loaded the packs, put the dogs on leashes, and headed up the trail.

Extremely strenuous does not begin to describe this particular trail. It traversed across several waterfalls without so much as a cable or handrail for support. At one point, we had to crawl through a hole in a rock to pick up the trail on the other side. But the most daunting part of all was when we came to a blockade of dirt and rock.

At first glance, it seemed as if the trail had abruptly ended.

To the left was the cliff edge of the mountain.

To the right was the wall of the mountain.

In front was a barricade of dirt, and behind was the way we had come.

Our poor shepherd, Mitch, who thinks he is the leader, was disoriented and confused. He couldn't figure out which way to go.

That's because he had never seen a ladder.

Yes, there on the right was a wooden ladder standing nearly eight feet tall. The trail went up, way up! As I looked at the ladder and then at the dogs, one question arose in my mind—*How in the world are we going to get a 90-pound shepherd and a 50-pound beagle up an eight-foot ladder?* The task seemed impossible, but what were our options? We could either figure out a way to continue our hike, or we could go back the way we had come and forsake the rest of the journey. Our ingenuity was certainly going to be put to the test.

With much hemming and hawing, coaxing and challenging, I finally got myself up the ladder. Jason grabbed Mitch, balanced him as best he could between the ladder and his own body and climbed up a couple of steps. From there, Mitch was able to use Jason as a push off point and bound to the top of the ladder where I awaited him. Tippy, our precious little beagle, is not one for bounding. Jason had to carry her all the way up the ladder.

Nevertheless, we made it, and there we stood, all four of us at the top of an eight-foot ladder. There were shorter ladders awaiting us further down the trail, but they didn't even slow us down, for the victory at the first ladder had served as a reminder of the very thing Gabriel told Mary—nothing is impossible with God!

MURDERED MIRACLES

Before we delve any further into the miraculous nature of Mary's conception, I would like to take a moment to point out that every conception and subsequent birth is a miracle. Unfortunately, we live in a world that pays little heed to this fact and feels no guilt or shame in killing over 115,000 babies every day. The miracle of life is tossed in a garbage can like a pair of old shoes, rejected and forgotten. But God does not forget, and each of those who have been so carelessly discarded have found comfort and acceptance in the arms of the loving Father.

As I was researching this chapter, I did an Internet search to see if I could locate the statistics for the number of abortions performed each day. What I came across were several sites calling themselves "abortion counters," and they served as just that. They kept track, in real time, of the number of abortions performed at any given moment. One could filter the number by region, date, or even how many abortions had taken place since reaching the website. The tallies blew my mind!

As I viewed the worldwide abortions, my heart sank to watch the numbers click by. At times, the statistics rose so quickly that the counter would literally skip numbers to keep up. The totals clicked by faster than the second hand on a clock. I don't know from where these websites get their information, nor do I know how accurate they are, but the entire thing truly sickened me. Although I am not a parent myself, I cannot understand how someone could do something so horrible. Abortion is murder, and it is wrong!

Can you imagine if Mary had decided to abort Jesus? If anyone had a reason to consider such a thing (not that I think anyone does), Mary did. I'm sure she was honored and that she felt unworthy of such an important role, but did her thoughts stop there?

By accepting such tidings, Mary was risking a lot. Think about it, she was an unwed woman, set to be married and carrying a child that did not belong to her intended spouse. Imagine the shame, the ridicule, the gossip. What would it be like to have your friends and family think the worst of you when you had, in truth, done nothing wrong? Was carrying the Son of God worth all of that?

Fortunately, Mary seemed to think so.

As soon as Gabriel was done speaking, Mary opened her mouth. *Behold the handmaid of the Lord; be it unto me according to thy word.* Mary declared, "I am the Lord's servant, and I will do whatever He asks of me."

Are we as willing to obey? When we see what our obedience will cost us, do we make excuses? A better question still is, do we have enough favor in God's sight that He would ask a favor of us to begin with? When He looks at us, what does He see?

An obedient servant?
A heart full of faith?
Or a partially devoted follower who turns the other way when the going gets tough?

Mary learned that when we trust and obey, God will work out all the details. When Joseph, her espoused, found out about her condition, he thought she had been unfaithful. Still, out of love and respect, he desired to break off the engagement privately so as not to embarrass her any further. But before he could go through with his plans, God sent His angel to explain the situation to Joseph. The wedding took place as planned, and life for the young couple appeared to be normal.

Well, as normal as could be when the Son of God was abiding in their home.

MIXED MESSAGES

I used to love Christmas time. There was something about decorating the house and listening to Christmas carols that made everything seem right with the world. And despite our small home and lack of finances, I always tried to do everything up big. Live tree in the corner. Garland around the door frames. The lighted village across the mantle. Decorative Christmas throws and pillows lined the couch. I even had special dishes for that festive time of year.

I designed and mailed out Christmas cards by the handful. But most of all, I looked forward to the shopping. Never one to settle for "just any old gift," I spent hours thinking long and hard about the perfect gift for each individual on my list. And I so looked forward to seeing the look on each person's face as he/she opened the gift I had so carefully selected.

Through the years, though, something has changed. Somehow my Tiny Tim mentality has been replaced with that of Ebenezer Scrooge. My decorations have dwindled down to a small tree and a few snowmen. I've stopped sending out Christmas cards altogether. I do most of my shopping online and fret much less about finding the perfect gifts. The thought of the church Christmas Cantata gives me a headache, and my holly, jolly Christmas feels like anything but. I've even been known to wish my way through the holidays so that life could get back to normal (whatever that is).

At first, I was baffled by the change in my behavior and attitude. But slowly, I began to realize what was happening. Christmas was becoming so commercialized that it was suffocating the joy of the season right out of me. I was growing frustrated with children and adults alike worrying about whether Santa would come without giving a moment's notice to the fact that Christ had. I became like Charlie Brown: "I think there must be something wrong with me, Linus. Christmas is coming, but I'm not happy. I don't feel the way I'm supposed to feel. . . I like getting presents and sending Christmas cards, and decorating trees and all that, but I'm still not happy. I always end up feeling depressed."

Please don't misunderstand. I don't have anything against Santa Claus or Rudolph or Frosty the Snowman. What bothers me is that we've become so fixated on them that we've lost sight of what Christmas is truly about. I want to celebrate a Christmas where it doesn't matter whether Santa comes. I want to celebrate Christmas as a reminder that Christ came to this earth in the form of a baby, so that He could live a sinless life and then die for my sins.

This world has been consumed by bitterness toward Christ and anything that represents Him. In my despair, I had allowed myself to become infected with a similar bitterness. Not toward the things of Christ, but rather toward their attitude. The outcome, however, was no different. The world focused on their commercialism, and I focused on the same. And all around the world, the miraculous birth of Christ was ignored.

A well-known television host recently commented, "I think commercialism helps Christmas, and I think that the more capitalism we can inject into the Christmas holiday the more spiritual I feel about it." Shortly after making this statement, he was quoted as saying, "There's a commercial break coming and I'm very excited about it, and you know why? Because that's what keeps daddy in suits."

The almighty dollar. Getting the newest toys. Keeping up with the Joneses. Buying love. Is this what Christmas has been reduced to? In the eyes of the world, I'm afraid so. But as for me, I agree with author Karen Kingsbury who said,

Christmas is ... a time to mark our progress through this earthly journey. Every December we can look back and marvel at the designs of God and realize how very little we are in control of the events that shaped the past year. Then, with hearts full, look to the celebration of that silent, holy night, and all its certainty. Because of Christmas, this we know: Christ was born for us. He is love and the plans he has for us always surpass those of our own.[2]

MIRACLE MINISTRY

The Bible actually doesn't have much to say about Jesus' earthly parents after His birth. We hear of Joseph during the trip to Jerusalem when Jesus is twelve, but that's the last we hear of him. Mentions of Mary are more numerous, but not very detailed. I think it is important, however, to notice that her role in Jesus' ministry did not stop at the miraculous birth.

And the third day there was a marriage in Cana of Galilee; and the mother of Jesus was there: And both Jesus was called, and his disciples, to the marriage. And when they wanted wine, the mother of Jesus saith unto him, They have no wine. Jesus saith unto her, Woman, what have I to do with thee? mine hour is not yet come. His mother saith unto the servants, Whatsoever he saith unto you, do it. And there were set there six waterpots of stone, after the manner of the purifying of the Jews, containing two or three firkins apiece. Jesus saith unto them, Fill the waterpots with water. And they filled them up to the brim. And he saith unto them, Draw out now, and bear unto the governor of the feast. And they bare it. When the ruler of the feast had tasted the water that was made wine, and knew not whence it was: (but the servants which drew the water knew;) the governor of the feast called the bridegroom, And saith unto him, Every man at the beginning doth set forth good wine; and when men have well drunk, then that which is worse: but thou hast kept the good wine until now. This

beginning of miracles did Jesus in Cana of Galilee, and
manifested forth his glory; and his disciples believed on
him. - (John 2:1-11)

Jason and I were engaged for fifteen months
before we got married. With both of us working full-time
and attending Bible college at night, it seemed wise to
give ourselves plenty of time for planning a wedding.
Not that I really needed that much time. Like most
females, I had been planning my wedding since I was a
little girl. Still, those fifteen months gave me plenty of
time to iron out all the details. As the wedding day drew
near, most everything was done, and while I had a few
concerns (mostly about the weather), there was one
worry that never crossed my mind.

I knew we would not run out of food!

After all, my grandmother was providing all the
food for the reception. To help you understand, picture a
family of five sitting before a small round table. Now,
shift your view from the table to the countertops
surrounding that table. See all of that food?

The chicken.
The meatloaf.
The steak.
The mashed potatoes.
The macaroni and cheese.
The potato salad.
The green beans.
The lima beans.
The rolls.
The pies.
The cookies.

Yes, that's all for that little family of five. For dinner.

Whether my grandmother is cooking for one or twenty, I never have to be concerned about having enough. Typically, my only concern is how to turn down the third helping of dinner without hurting her feelings. That and wondering where I'm going to find clothes that will fit me by the time I return home.

Sure enough, after everyone at our wedding reception had eaten their fill. . .and then some, there was enough food left over for another wedding reception. My lack of concern was justified.

I wonder if this couple at Cana were so calm. Did they worry about the weather raining out their lovely event? Were they concerned that someone wouldn't arrive on time? Did they even contemplate what they would do if they ran out of wine? Or was it possible that the thought never dawned on them? Let's face it. We're not exactly thinking our best on our wedding day, now are we? We're so twitterpated (as they say in "Bambi") that we can't even remember our own names.

Whatever their doubts or certainties, they did run out of wine. Whether the bride and bridegroom knew this, we're left to wonder. But Mary knew. Not only did she know of the problem, but she also knew of the solution.

Look at the simplicity of Mary's statement. "They have no wine." She didn't worry. She didn't try to solve the problem herself. She didn't even ask Jesus to do anything. No, she modeled for us the perfect formula for dealing with any problem in our lives. She told Jesus about the problem and then left it up to Him to solve it as He would.

What I find very interesting about Mary's behavior is that, as far as we know, Jesus had never performed a miracle up to this point. How did Mary know He could? What made Mary so sure that Jesus could solve the problem?

Immediately following Jesus' birth, the Bible tells us that *Mary kept all these things, and pondered them in her heart.*[3]

What things? I think one of the things she kept and pondered was the statement of Gabriel, *For with God nothing shall be impossible.* Mary knew that Jesus was God in the flesh, so she put her faith in her Son and left the results up to Him. . .sort of.

When Mary told Jesus of the predicament, Jesus answered her, *Woman, what have I to do with thee? mine hour is not yet come.* From our finite standpoint, it seems as if Jesus was disrespectful or harsh, but we know that isn't the case. I think Jesus was merely reminding his mother that He was subject to His Father's instructions and timeline, not hers. Perhaps, He was merely testing her faith.

And if that be the case, Mary passed with flying colors, for her next words are to the servants, *Whatsoever he saith unto you, do it.*

That has to be the most important instruction any of us could ever give or receive. It sounds so simple, yet it is not simple at all. We long to be like the servants who heard Jesus' instructions to fill the pots with water and then hastened to obey. Yet, we're so consumed with our own questions and curiosities, we can't seem to move past them.

When Jesus tells us to do something, we want to know why.

What's the plan, Lord?

How are you going to work this out?

May I see the blueprints, please?

Why can't we trust and do what we're told? What makes us think that God owes us an explanation? Why can't we exhibit the kind of faith that Mary and the servants had on that day? Even when Jesus told the servants to draw out some of the water and take it to the governor, they didn't hesitate. On the surface, that doesn't seem like a big deal, but let me set the scene.

The Bible states that the water pots were after the manner of the purifying of the Jews. The best I can figure is that those water pots were the ones that held the water for washing the feet of the guests after they had walked for miles on the dusty roads. Jesus wants the servants to take these pots that have had dirty feet water in them and fill them with fresh water. Then, He wants them to take a cup of this water to the most important guest of all, the governor (who, of course, would be expecting wine). Do you see now why their faith must have been grand? Would you want to walk up to the governor and hand him a cup of dirty feet water? No, I didn't think so.

My question is, were Mary or the servants surprised when the governor stood up and declared that the wine was the best that had been served the entire feast? Did they look at each other with stunned faces? Or did they simply look at Jesus in awe, captivated by One who could turn water into wine without so much as a word?

I can't help wondering what would have happened at the wedding if Mary had kept silent. Would Jesus have still turned the water into wine? After all, He said it wasn't time yet. Would the first miracle in Jesus' earthly ministry have occurred at the wedding in Cana? And most important of all, how many lives were touched that day when Mary, once again, allowed herself to be part of God's plan?

Most of us need an example like Mary's to help us believe God can use us in any significant way. We have no trouble believing God can use others, but when we look at ourselves, all we can see is our inadequacies and inabilities. So, clinging white-knuckled to our comfort zones, we tend to stick with what comes naturally. We shrink back from God's upward call and find ourselves reluctant to say, "Yes, Lord! I'm Your servant. Use me as You please!" . . .Yet, uncomfortable as it may be for us, God steers us in those directions for our own good. He does it so He can shine on us, in us, and through us into the lives of others. And I've found that by leaning into His plans, we can always find the greatest joy.[4]

Chapter Four:

JAILHOUSE ROCK

And it came to pass, as we went to prayer, a certain damsel possessed with a spirit of divination met us, which brought her masters much gain by soothsaying: The same followed Paul and us, and cried, saying, These men are the servants of the most high God, which shew unto us the way of salvation. And this did she many days. But Paul, being grieved, turned and said to the spirit, I command thee in the name of Jesus Christ to come out of her. And he came out the same hour. And when her masters saw that the hope of their gains was gone, they caught Paul and Silas, and drew them into the marketplace unto the rulers, And brought them to the magistrates, saying, These men, being Jews, do exceedingly trouble our city, And teach customs, which are not lawful for us to receive, neither to observe, being Romans. And the multitude rose up together against them: and the magistrates rent off their clothes, and commanded to beat them. And when they had laid many stripes upon them, they cast them into prison, charging the jailor to keep them safely: Who, having received such a charge, thrust them into the inner prison, and made their feet fast in the stocks. And at midnight Paul and Silas prayed, and sang praises unto God: and the prisoners heard them. And suddenly there was a great earthquake, so that the foundations of the prison were shaken: and immediately all the doors were opened, and every one's bands were loosed. And the keeper of the prison awaking out of his sleep, and seeing the prison doors open, he drew out his sword, and would have killed himself, supposing that the prisoners had been fled. But Paul cried with a loud voice, saying, Do thyself no harm: for we are all here. Then he called for a light, and sprang in, and came trembling, and fell down before Paul and Silas, And brought them out, and said, Sirs, what must I do to be saved? And they said, Believe on the Lord Jesus Christ, and thou shalt be saved, and thy house. And they spake unto him the word of the Lord, and to all that were in his house. And he took them the same hour of the night, and washed their stripes; and was baptized, he and all his, straightway. And when he had brought them into his house, he set meat before them, and rejoiced, believing in God with all his house. - Acts 16:16-34

As Christians, it sometimes seems like the harder we try to serve God, the more trouble arises. But if you think about it, doesn't that only make sense? If we're following the Lord's will and doing what He's asked of us, we can be assured that Satan will fight us every step of the way. Why does he need to waste his time and effort on those who aren't serving? They're already right where he wants them. No, he has a different target. He wants to distract those who are faithful. He wants to discourage those who are striving to do right. He wants to defeat those who are heeding the voice of God. I Peter 5:8 cautions us, *Be sober, be vigilant; because your adversary the devil, as a roaring lion, walketh about, seeking whom he may devour.*

Just before writing this chapter, he attacked me with a vengeance. I had taken my computer to church on Sunday morning to record my Sunday school lesson as usual. After the lesson, I shut my computer down, placed it in its bag, and carried it home. When I went to set the computer up that evening, however, I was dismayed to discover that it would not boot up. Yes, my computer that had been running smoothly that very morning was totally uncooperative. After a week of trying different things to correct the problem, we finally determined that the only solution was to wipe the computer clean and start from scratch. Thankfully, I was able to recover my documents and programs before wiping the system clean. But still, the computer crash cost a lot of time and effort.

During that overwhelming process, I had to keep reminding myself that all things work together for good to those who love God. I had to remind myself that God is not cruel or unkind. When I wanted to complain, "Lord, I'm trying to serve You. Why would You allow this to happen? Why are You making it more difficult for me to do Your will?" the Lord reminded me that all suffering has a purpose.

In our story in Acts, Paul and Silas were, no doubt, in the will of the Lord. Nevertheless, they became victim to the roaring lion himself. When Paul cast the demons out of the young girl, her masters were outraged. They had been using this poor girl to make money. I don't even like to imagine what they required of her beyond her ability to tell the future. We have every reason to believe they were cruel and offered her no hospitality. From the look of things, she was a prisoner, both of the demons and of her masters. But Paul, through the power of God, released her from her prison, knowing it could very well lead him to a prison of his own.

In their fury, these men lashed out at Paul and Silas. And to ensure they were properly punished, the masters went so far as to make false accusations against them. If there's one thing we can always count on, it's that the devil's crowd will mimic his behavior. The Bible says that Satan is the father of all lies, so it is only natural to conclude that his children would use lies to their advantage as well. That's not to say that Christians never lie. Sadly, great harm has often been inflicted by the lies of a Christian. Hopefully, those Christians felt remorse and made things right. These masters, on the other hand, were only too happy to stand by and watch as Paul and Silas were beaten and imprisoned for crimes they hadn't committed.

Delight in the Darkness

At six o'clock this morning, I was awakened by the sound of not one or two, but an entire choir of whippoorwills. (If you've never heard a whippoorwill, it sounds a lot like an owl on steroids.) From the sound of it, the ensemble was directly outside my bedroom window. One would call out, and the others would answer. At first, I felt privileged to listen to the melodic conversation, but when it went on and on, I became agitated. It was, after all, only six o'clock in the morning, and Jason hadn't gotten home from work until after two o'clock. I'm no math whiz, but I can tell you right now that *that* amount of sleep is not enough for me.

For nearly half an hour I listened to the sound of the whippoorwills. At one point, I wanted to open my window and scream into the darkness, "This is not the time for choir practice!" Thankfully, they quieted down before I did so.

Later on, after I had time to wake up and shake off my grumbles, I realized how foolish my behavior and attitude had been. What right did I have to begrudge the birds their song simply because I wasn't ready to get out of bed yet? In fact, the more I thought about it, the more I realized that I had been wrong, not only in my attitude but also in the words that nearly tumbled from my mouth.

Anytime is a good time for choir practice!

The whippoorwills were simply carrying out the command issued over and over again in the Bible—sing unto the Lord. They had something to say, and they didn't hold back. They had a song in their hearts, so they let it fly. Isn't that what we're supposed to do? Isn't that what the Bible instructs? Don't we have something worth singing about?

Now I understand that some people are more prone to sing than others. I also understand that some people enjoy singing while those around them wished sincerely that they didn't. I wouldn't say these people are tone deaf, but their song can only be described as a joyful noise. But you know what? That's okay. God would rather hear that joyful noise than to see a saint without a song. He longs to hear our praise, and He deserves our worship!

As we abide in Christ, trust Him, and depend on His grace, we always have something to sing about.[1]

Paul and Silas understood that. Exhausted, wounded and weary, the missionaries found delight in the darkness of the dungeon. They didn't throw a pity party. They didn't complain or contemplate defeat. No, they prayed and sang.

And I don't believe their song was "Nobody Knows the Trouble I've Seen."

In fact, I believe their song might have closely resembled "Praise You in This Storm" or "Great Is Thy Faithfulness." Whatever their song, it was not a soothing humming. The Bible says it was loud enough that all the prisoners heard. (We can only hope the duo were not in the "joyful noise club," lest the other prisoners think the midnight serenade was part of their punishment.)

Corrie ten Boom once stated, *When you're covered by His wings, it can get pretty dark.* Yes, in His wings there is safety, but that doesn't mean there will be no darkness. Nevertheless, like Paul and Silas, we, too, can find delight in our dungeons of darkness. To do so, we need only use the same approach they did.

DIRECT YOUR DEMEANOR

First, we must focus on Christ and not the crisis. The more we focus on the problem, the bigger it appears. Likewise, the more we focus on God, the bigger He appears. I'm reminded of a lesson God prepared for me about this very topic.

A couple of weeks ago, I was running an errand that required me to drive farther than I'm usually comfortable with. I don't like to drive. I know how to drive, and I'm very competent, I just don't enjoy it. In addition to that, I inherited my dad's sense of direction, which means I couldn't find my way out of a paper bag with an opening at both ends. Nevertheless, I had an errand that needed to be run, so I hopped in the truck and followed the directions my husband had given me. I had driven to the place a couple of times before, so I knew it wasn't that difficult. It was the trip home that gave me trouble.

As I drove, I was listening to a book on CD. In fact, I was engrossed in the story. A little too engrossed as it turns out. Don't get me wrong, I was watching where I was going and paying attention to traffic. What I didn't notice, however, was that I missed a turn. Slowly, as I drove along, I realized that nothing looked familiar anymore. The farther I went, the less familiar things looked. In a state of panic, I realized what I had done. It was impossible for me to determine, however, how far past my turn I had gone. I was debating whether to turn around and try to find my turn or continue on in hopes that something would become familiar.

I continued down the road, glancing around, searching for anything that looked familiar. I tried to calm my churning stomach, telling myself that I could always turn around and go back the other way. But then, a moment of decision appeared. The road I was on no longer went straight. All traffic had to turn either left or right. I reasoned that since I was supposed to have turned left a ways back, turning left would be the correct choice. In the back of my mind, I prayed that reasoning was sound. Before long, I began to see signs for the BiLo Center, which is very close to my house. Relieved, I followed the signs, knowing that I could find my way home from there.

Looking back, it's a humorous tale. At the time, however, I was not laughing. Thankfully, my distraction only cost me a little time and panic. It could have been much worse.

Distraction is a deadly tool used by Satan to get us off course in our Christian walk. Often, we are so distracted that we don't even realize we're off course until we're far from where we should be. Then we're left stumbling around in the dark, trying to figure out where we took the wrong turn and how to get back on track.

Many things can serve as a distraction: people, circumstances, money, fame, and sin, just to name a few. These things (except sin), in and of themselves, are not wrong. But our focus on them can be. It's easy to get so bogged down with certain things that we lose our true focus. We get off course. In short, we miss our turn.

Distraction. It seems innocent, but it's so very deadly! So how can we fight against it? I think it's best said in Joshua 1:8: *This book of the law shall not depart out of thy mouth; but thou shalt meditate therein day and night, that thou mayest observe to do according to all that is written therein: for then thou shalt make thy way prosperous, and then thou shalt have good success.*

It's hard to be distracted when we're meditating on God's Word. By focusing on the message of the Bible day and night, we won't be so easily swayed by other things that come along. Instead, God's Word will direct our eyes to Christ, and as long as we're looking to Him, we're headed in the right direction. It's simply a matter of focus.

DAZZLING DISTRESS

Second, we can delight in the fact that we can identify with Jesus through our suffering. Our trials and afflictions give us just a small taste of what Jesus went through to ensure us a place with Him for all eternity. That realization alone ought to give us the strength to suffer more for Him. Just ask Peter Xu Yongze, the founder of one of the largest religious movements in China.

According to the Chinese Constitution, "Citizens of the People's Republic of China enjoy the freedom of religious belief." Beijing backed up that statement in 1997, saying, "In China, no one is to be punished due to their religious belief." But Mr. Xu can attest that, sadly, such is not the case. Xu was imprisoned five times and spent a total of eight years in Chinese prisons for sharing the gospel of Christ.

"They say you can believe, but you can't evangelize," Mr. Xu said. "But that is a natural act for Christians. The Bible commands us to preach the gospel."

Despite the opposition and myriad of threats, Christianity is increasing in China by leaps and bounds. This is, in part, because of the valiant efforts of people like Mr. Xu, who understand the joy of sharing in Christ's suffering and doing His will no matter what. His response to his fifth imprisonment was, "Thanks to God's grace, I have become the companion with all saints in the suffering and kingdom and patient endurance that are ours in Jesus."

Mr. Xu is currently living in the United States and is the founder of the Back to Jerusalem Gospel Mission. As it has been since he received his call to preach, his main goal is to evangelize and send the Gospel to the unreached population across the world, including Asia.

Matthew 10:28 says, *And fear not them which kill the body, but are not able to kill the soul: but rather fear him which is able to destroy both soul and body in hell.*

Psalm 56:11 tells us, *In God have I put my trust: I will not be afraid what man can do unto me.*

And Psalm 118:6 reminds us, *The Lord is on my side; I will not fear: what can man do unto me?*

All three of these verses carry the same message: we need not fear physical suffering. If God is on our side (which He is if we are His children), then we have no reason to be afraid. Yes, the suffering will be unpleasant, but we have the promise that it will be worth it. Not only did Paul and Silas know this truth, but they believed it and acted according to that belief.

DISMISSED DOUBTS

Third, we need to believe that God is in control. Nothing will happen to us that He does not allow. His will *will* be done, and isn't the fulfillment of His will the outcome we desire? One way or another, He will deliver us. The delivery method, however, is up to Him.

He delivered Noah and his family from the flood.

He delivered Lot and his daughters from Sodom and Gomorrah.

He delivered David from Saul's fury, but only after months of fleeing for his life.

He delivered Daniel from the lion's den and Shadrach, Meshach, and Abednego from the fiery furnace, but He did not prevent them from being tormented in the first place.

He delivered Peter from prison and James into heaven.

He delivered Lazarus from the grave but did not deliver Jesus from the pain and suffering of the cross.

We cannot hope to understand His ways, but we can trust that He knows best.

It is just as important to trust God as it is to obey Him. When we disobey God, we defy His authority and despise His holiness. But when we fail to trust God we doubt His sovereignty and question His goodness. In those cases, we cast aspersions upon His majesty and

His character. God views our distrust of Him as seriously as He views our disobedience. [2]

On this occasion, God chose to send an earthquake to rattle open the prison doors, and while He was at it, He unbound all the chains. I think it's interesting to note the different approach to this prison break in comparison to Peter's prison break a couple of chapters back. In Peter's rescue, he had a personal angel to help him and lead him out of the prison. Paul and Silas had no such companion, but then again, they weren't drowsy from slumber, so perhaps they didn't need one. Whatever the case, it serves to reinforce the truth that God works in numerous ways. Just because He meets a need one way in a particular situation doesn't mean He'll meet the need in the same way at another time. Take Moses, for example. While leading the children of Israel through the wilderness, Moses was once instructed to hit a rock to acquire water while another time he was instructed to speak to the rock. In the New Testament, when Jesus healed the lepers, each time varied. Sometimes he spoke to them while other times he actually touched them. The point is this: God knows the best way to accomplish His will. If He is willing to perform a miracle on our behalf, who are we to question how He brings that miracle about?

DECISIONS DURING DELIVERANCE

Another thing that intrigues me at this point in the story is a detail that I didn't notice for many years of Bible reading and study. Once again, I place myself in Paul's shoes (or Silas', depending on which one had smaller feet). I'm in prison. I'm tired and weary, but still, I'm praising God. I hear a low rumble, and the earth all around begins to shake. The cell doors swing open, and the shackles on my hands and feet fall to the ground. My response? "God truly does respond to the praises of His people." And with that, I would have made a run for it. After all, the miraculous events could not have been mere coincidence or accident. It had to be the work of God. "God wants me to go free!"

But Paul and Silas must have been so in tune with God that even with their freedom on the line, they knew God's will was for them to remain where they were. And there they sat with nothing holding them there except their desire to do God's will. That amazes me, but what amazes me more is the realization that Paul and Silas were not the only prisoners freed that night. According to the Bible, all the doors were opened, and all the chains were loosed, yet none of the prisoners fled. Talk about an overlooked miracle! Here we have a ragtag group of prisoners, likely imprisoned for life or facing a death sentence. The chances are that most of them were justly convicted. Surely, each of them would have jumped at the chance to taste freedom. Yet they remained.

I appreciate that God doesn't give us all the details in the Bible. I like how He leaves some of the "minor" facts out so that we must use our imaginations to fill in the blanks. I don't know about you, but I have a great imagination! I love to fill in the blanks, and I have some pretty good ideas about why the prisoners didn't flee, but for the sake of time, I'll share with you my favorite.

Do you remember the angels and the flaming sword that God placed in front of the entrance to the Garden of Eden after Adam and Eve sinned? I like to think that every cell (except for the one for Paul and Silas) had one of those angels guarding the entrance. Yes, the bands were loosed. Yes, the doors were open. But who's to say there wasn't a grinning angel standing in each doorway and saying, "Go ahead, make my day"? (I told you I had a good imagination!)

Regardless of how it happened, nobody escaped the prison that night despite the fact that there were no obvious obstacles to prevent it. When God has a plan, nothing can thwart it. And the object of God's plan was about to make his grand entrance.

DESPAIR IN THE DOORWAY

And the keeper of the prison awaking out of his sleep, and seeing the prison doors open, he drew out his sword, and would have killed himself, supposing that the prisoners had been fled. (Acts 16:27)

Poor guy! He was just trying to do his job, although I don't think he was actually supposed to be sleeping, but that's a thought for another day. This unfortunate soldier was awakened from his sleep, no doubt by the earthquake, and the first thing he noticed was that all the cell doors were standing open. Naturally, he assumed the prisoners had escaped. Why wouldn't they? Why, indeed! In his forlorn state, his first instinct was to take out his sword and end his life.

The problem with suicide is that it is a permanent solution to a temporary problem, yet sadly it is the only solution some can see when surrounded by darkness. Statistics show that suicide is attempted once every 40 seconds in the US alone. For a myriad of reasons, people see death as their only option or escape. The Philippian jailer felt the same way. We can only imagine the thoughts that must have been running rampant through his mind, but I feel they were thoughts to which many of us can relate.

I'm such a failure. Despite his desire to do his job, the jailer thought he had failed, and failure is a powerful thing. It can sap us of our strength and our joy. It can bring about feelings of worthlessness. It is a popular tool in Satan's workshop, one that has proven its effectiveness. It's a shame the jailer didn't have the words of Winston Churchill, "Success is not final, failure is not fatal: it is the courage to continue that counts." Yes, failure is hard. Sure, it's difficult to get back up, dust ourselves off, and try again. But our effort is not in vain, and we must remember that we are not walking alone.

I don't want to embarrass my family. I often wonder how many times these have been someone's last words. They messed up (as we are all prone to do), but rather than bring disgrace to their family, they decided to end it all. The cause seems noble, but I guarantee you that if you asked that person's loved ones what they thought about it, they would tell you that they would much rather have lived with the shame than with the loss of their loved one. In the heat of the moment, in the midnight hour, everything seems so dark and hopeless. That is not the time to make a decision. Wait for the dawn. If the jailer had waited until the light of dawn filled the prison, he would have seen that the prisoners were still there. He wouldn't have needed Paul's intervention. No matter how hopeless the situation may seem, give it time, and talk to your family. I'm sure they're willing to walk the road with you.

I have nothing left to live for. At this point, the jailer realized that as soon as his superiors found out the prisoners had escaped, they were going to kill him. Mercy was not shown to those who failed to do their jobs. From the jailer's point of view, there was no reason to live. What he didn't see, however, was God's point of view. God wasn't done with this man. He still had a plan, a job that only this man could accomplish. From God's point of view, the jailer had so much to live for. When it seems as if you've lost everything and there's nothing worth living for, remember that you only see one point of view. God still has a plan for you. He's not done with you yet. He has a job that only you can do, and He'll give you everything you need to accomplish that job. Don't quit on God. He didn't quit on you.

DIRECTIONS FROM THE DIVINE

Before the jailer could end his life, Paul intervened and assured the man that all the prisoners were still in the prison. The jailer called for a light to see for himself that all was as Paul had said. Relieved, yet convicted, he fell down at the feet of the duo and inquired, "What must I do to be saved?" Evidently, the Holy Spirit had been working on the heart of the jailer during the midnight hour. He had seen enough. He had heard enough. He knew what he needed, but he required someone to show him the way.

Paul's response was simple and direct. In fact, the verse is one of the memory verses I taught my kindergartners when I was a teacher. Why? Because it is a simple, understandable verse that shows the way to salvation. *Believe on the Lord Jesus Christ, and thou shalt be saved.*[3]

The path to Heaven, plain and simple. Believe! Not baptism. Not works. Not wealth. Believe in Christ and accept Him as Lord of your life. Yes, salvation is truly that simple. The jailer heeded the instructions, and as we see at the end of the passage, he and his entire family were converted. None of which would have happened if God's plan had not taken place. God needed Paul and Silas in that prison so they could witness to the jailer, so he, in turn, could be a witness to his family. And I doubt the influence ended there. No, I have a feeling that influence spread like wildfire, and many souls were saved because Paul and Silas were willing to be used by God in a miraculous way.

Many of us long to be used by God, but we have our own plans and ambitions about how we want to be used. We picture ourselves as little David standing bravely before the giant or as Joshua marching around the walls of Jericho. We bask in the possibility of being able to heal the sick or raise the dead. We're willing to stretch our necks out a little, but we would really rather not stray too far from our comfort zones. After all, life is tough enough.

But God needs servants who are willing to be used in the darkest dungeons. He needs those who are willing to go where there is no light to share the light of His love. He needs those who are so in tune with Him that they don't just settle for the obvious but heed His word, even if it means denying themselves. He needs another Paul, another Silas. Are we willing to heed His call?

The benefits of trusting the Lord may be deferred, but they're always worth the wait.[4]

Section Three: Miracles of Healing

HE'S STILL WORKING MIRACLES

Chapter Five:

A Tale of Two Miracles

And, behold, there cometh one of the rulers of the synagogue, Jairus by name; and when he saw him, he fell at his feet, And besought him greatly, saying, My little daughter lieth at the point of death: I pray thee, come and lay thy hands on her, that she may be healed; and she shall live. And Jesus went with him; and much people followed him, and thronged him. And a certain woman, which had an issue of blood twelve years, And had suffered many things of many physicians, and had spent all that she had, and was nothing bettered, but rather grew worse, When she had heard of Jesus, came in the press behind, and touched his garment. For she said, If I may touch but his clothes, I shall be whole. And straightway the fountain of her blood was dried up; and she felt in her body that she was healed of that plague. And Jesus, immediately knowing in himself that virtue had gone out of him, turned him about in the press, and said, Who touched my clothes? And his disciples said unto him, Thou seest the multitude thronging thee, and sayest thou, Who touched me? And he looked round about to see her that had done this thing. But the woman fearing and trembling, knowing what was done in her, came and fell down before him, and told him all the truth. And he said unto her, Daughter, thy faith hath made thee whole; go in peace, and be whole of thy plague. While he yet spake, there came from the ruler of the synagogue's house certain which said, Thy daughter is dead: why troublest thou the Master any further? As soon as Jesus heard the word that was spoken, he saith unto the ruler of the synagogue, Be not afraid, only believe. - Mark 5:22-36

Here we have a story like no other in the Bible in that it is the tale of two miracles intertwined within a story of love and compassion. On the surface, the two miracles seem unrelated except for the fact that they occur within moments of each other, but are they really? Could it be that three of the four gospels tell of these events because there is an abundance of resounding truths to be found within their unfolding? I can think of no better way to find out than to make acquaintances with the main characters. Naturally, one would assume that we would begin with Jairus. After all, he was a rich ruler. He was famous, important, a man of high standing. But even though he is mentioned first in the Scriptures, the story actually begins with the unnamed woman, for it is she who had suffered the longest.

To understand the plight of this woman, we must look beyond the surface of her illness. It's one thing to know that she was sick and suffering from a disease. It's quite another to understand the impact that sickness had on her life. Physically, this woman was tired, frail and weak. Financially, she was ruined. She had spent every dime she had on doctors and treatments, to no avail. In fact, she was worse off for her efforts. Socially, she was an outcast. A woman in her state was considered unclean, no better than a leper. Everything and everyone she touched immediately became unclean. If she had a husband, she could not kiss or hug him. If she had children, she could not hold or comfort them. And this woman had suffered for twelve years. Can you imagine twelve years without the simplest touch from someone dear to you? As if all of that weren't bad enough, the woman was spiritually malnourished, for she was not allowed to worship in the house of God. Essentially, she was cut off from everyone, destined to live out the remainder of her life in isolation and shame. Lonely. Helpless. Hopeless. Desperate.

Then one day she heard about a man who could heal the sick. From all accounts, she could tell that this man wasn't any ordinary healer. In fact, from what she'd heard, there wasn't anything ordinary about Him. And despite her repeated failures, she dared to hope that this man held the key to her physical and emotional prison. It was that reborn hope, I believe, that gave her the strength and courage to venture from her home that day. Lumbering through the streets, careful not to draw attention to herself, she followed the throng and came face to face with a life-altering decision.

Deep down, she firmly believed that if she could simply touch the hem of Jesus' garment, she would be healed, but at what cost? Imagine the multitude of thoughts that must have been running through this poor woman's mind as she pressed through the crowd. *What if someone recognizes me before I reach Him? What will Jesus do to me when He realizes that my touch has rendered Him unclean? Will my touch hinder Him from saving the little girl He's on His way to heal? How much longer can I live this way?* I love the way author Sheila Walsh describes it.

The woman pauses. She has no rights here. She shouldn't even be here. She is unclean, untouchable. Anyone or anything who touches her will also be unclean, untouchable for at least seven days. Plus, she can't ask Jesus to help her before He goes to the house of Capernaum's lead rabbi, whose twelve-year-old daughter was dying! She was the antitheses of Jairus's daughter, who was loved, fought for, treasured, her whole life ahead of her. No one fought for this woman anymore. She had no champion.[1]

Or did she?

Before her fear overwhelmed her, she reached out to Jesus in a determination born of desperation. Crawling on the ground, she stretched out her hand and grasped the hem of His robe. And at that moment, everything changed. The pain was gone. The weariness disappeared. The blood stopped flowing, and adrenaline started surging. I imagine the woman could have leaped for joy, but instead, she quietly backed into the crowd, willing to bask alone in her healing. However, Jesus wasn't finished with this woman.

HEALING AND HESITATION

In the midst of the commotion, Jesus paused and turned, the crowd stopping on his heels and following His gaze. "Who touched me?" He questioned, as if He didn't know. The disciples were incredulous. "You're kidding, right? I mean, look at all these people. They're everywhere, pushing and shoving just to be near you. And you want to know who touched you? Who didn't touch you?" I have to agree with the disciples on this one. It does seem like a ludicrous question considering the circumstances. However, I have a question of my own. Of all the people touching Jesus that day, why is there only record of one healing? There is no doubt in my mind that at least half of the people there with Him that day were there for healing. We see the truth of that scattered all through the gospels. So if they all came, and they all touched, why weren't they all healed? Why did Jesus only single out this one touch? It could be that the others wanted healing but weren't expecting healing as this woman was. I don't know, but it's an intriguing question, don't you think? As for Jesus' inquiry, He wasn't asking it for the sake of the disciples or to appease His own curiosity. He was asking on behalf of the woman. Whether she knew it at the time or not, she needed Him to ask.

By slipping back into the crowd with her stolen miracle, the woman would have missed out on the other blessings Jesus had to offer. He wasn't only interested in her physical healing. He had a bigger plan, a higher goal. He wanted to offer her spiritual healing and a restoration of her place in society. He wanted to give her a new life, but it was up to her to step up and claim it.

But the woman fearing and trembling, knowing what was done in her, came and fell down before him, and told him all the truth. (Mark 5:33)

Once again, fear gripped her heart. She knew what she'd done. She knew that He knew what she'd done. She could have run away. She could have continued back through the crowd. But something compelled her to stumble forward and spill out her tale. Tears of past pain and rejection mingled with those of joy and relief as she explained to Jesus and the onlooking crowd why she had touched Him. The crowd waited with bated breath to see what Jesus would say and do to this burden of society. Would He command that the crowd stone her for her boldness and defiance of the law? Would He see that she was imprisoned or banished to a land far away? No, as always, Jesus was true to His nature.

And he said unto her, Daughter, thy faith hath made thee whole; go in peace, and be whole of thy plague. (Mark 5:34)

Do you realize that this is the only time in the Bible that Jesus referred to a woman as "daughter"? Of all the women Jesus knew and considered friends, this unknown lawbreaker received a great honor from the lips of her Savior. The elation that filled this woman's heart at that moment must have been nearly uncontainable. For twelve years, she had lived a life of ridicule—unclean, poor, wretched, common, unknown. And now, in the blink of an eye, all of those labels were torn away and replaced with a single title: *daughter*. Because of her faith, she walked away that day with so much more than she had asked for. In fact, she hadn't really asked for anything, but that didn't stop Jesus from allowing her to have it. His healing power didn't accidentally slip away from Him. He allowed it to flow to this woman who needed more than what she currently sought. Even in His haste and busy schedule, He saw the opportunity to touch one more life, and He took it.

What initially seemed an embarrassing scene actually restored the woman to her rightful standing. There was no doubt of her cleansing. Jesus had proclaimed her healed. Jesus had praised her faith. He had sent her on her way. She instantly regained her membership into society. Meanwhile, Jairus was losing his patience. After all, Jesus had been on the way to heal his daughter. She was dying. She needed help. While I don't think Jairus begrudged this woman her healing, he had other priorities. But things were about to change.

GRIEF AND DESPAIR

While he yet spake, there came from the ruler of the synagogue's house certain which said, Thy daughter is dead: why troublest thou the Master any further? (Mark 5:35)

Dead? It's every parent's worst nightmare. While she was alive, there was hope, but now. . . I have to wonder which emotion welled up the most in Jairus at that moment—grief for his lost daughter or anger at the woman who had taken up Jesus' time on the road to Jairus' house. A few minutes could have meant the difference between life and death for this little girl. Anyone who's suffered grief will tell you that the need to blame someone or something is greatest in the darkest hour. But before Jairus could say or do anything, Jesus attempted to set his mind and heart at ease.

As soon as Jesus heard the word that was spoken, he saith unto the ruler of the synagogue, Be not afraid, only believe. And he suffered no man to follow him, save Peter, and James, and John the brother of James. And he cometh to the house of the ruler of the synagogue, and seeth the tumult, and them that wept and wailed greatly. And when he was come in, he saith unto them, Why make ye this ado, and weep? the damsel is not dead, but sleepeth. And they laughed him to scorn. But when he had put them all out, he taketh the father and the mother of the damsel, and them that were with him, and entereth in where the damsel was lying. And he took the damsel by the hand, and said unto her, Talitha cumi; which is, being interpreted, Damsel, I say unto thee, arise. And straightway the damsel arose, and walked; for she was of the age of twelve years. And they were astonished with a great astonishment. And he charged them straitly that no man should know it; and commanded that something should be given her to eat. (Mark 5:36-43)

The Bible describes the scene at Jairus' house as a tumult. The word *tumult* can be defined as confusion or disorder. Picture the scene that Jesus walked into. Crowds of people standing everywhere. The heart-breaking sobs of the mourners. Sadness. Despair. Confusion. And I imagine a few guilt-laden glances toward Jesus. From their perspective, He was late. He should have hurried. He should have dropped everything for this important ruler, for this precious child. As if their accusations weren't bad enough, they then had the nerve to ridicule Him for His proclamation that the girl was not dead. Get this now. It's too important to overlook. The Giver of Life had made a statement concerning life. How dare they laugh at Him! How dare we!

Too often in life, we allow ourselves to think that we know better than God. While we may not laugh at His proclamations, we push them aside and carry on with our own plans and desires. We fool ourselves into thinking that our ways, which seem logical and thought-out, are the means to dealing with our current situation. God's ways, on the other hand, make no sense. Die to live? Give so that it can be given unto you? Suffer to receive peace? Our finite minds simply can't comprehend how such tactics will get us through our predicament, so we ignore them and do it our own way. If Jesus had allowed this crowd to get away with that, the little girl would have never drawn another breath. They would have prevented a miracle from taking place. How many times does our obstinacy prevent miracles from taking place in our own lives? I shudder to think.

Not wanting to be surrounded by such a crowd of gloomy guses, Jesus sent the people out of the house, allowing only Jairus, his wife, and the three disciples to accompany Him. He held the pale, limp hand in His and spoke with both love and compassion. *Damsel, I say unto thee, arise.* Notice the title, "damsel," not "daughter" as with the woman with the issue of blood. At the sound of His voice, the girl immediately sat up. She couldn't help herself, for His voice was one she could not resist. As the Bible tells us, even death could not separate her from the love of God. She went from still and lifeless to up and walking around in a matter of minutes.

If I've had a bad cold or a headache, it takes a little while before I feel strong enough to be up and walking. After a particularly bad migraine, it takes nearly a week before I feel like myself again. This poor child had been dead! One would think she would be tired or weak, but the Scriptures give no indication of that. In fact, the Bible tells us that she was strong enough to eat. It was like she had just risen from a good nap.

WHAT'S IN A NUMBER?

I find it interesting that two of the three gospels that tell this story make a point of telling us the age of this little girl as well as the number of years that the woman with the issue of blood had suffered. Twelve years. Coincidence? I mean, really, what are the chances that such a thing would occur to two people who had nothing in common except that each received healing from Jesus? Think about it. For the twelve years that this little girl had been loved and cherished, the woman had been forsaken and cast aside. For the twelve years that the little girl enjoyed life and basked in the family's riches, the woman had endured life and lived in poverty, reaching the depths where she had not even been able to scrape together enough money for a doctor's visit.

At the beginning of this chapter, I told you how I believe the tale of these two miracles were intertwined for a reason, and that reason is this: God is not a respecter of persons. In other words, He doesn't play favorites. He cares for the wealthy, the influential, the powerful, but He also cares for the despicable, the poor, the lowly. He loves both the lovable and the unlovable, the wanted and the unwanted, the clean and the unclean. The reason that He can display such love is that, in His eyes, there's no such thing as unlovable or unwanted. God looks at people through a different lens than we do. You might say that He views us through rose-colored glasses, but it goes so far beyond that. When God looks at us, it is through glasses stained crimson by the blood of His Son, Jesus Christ. Because of His sacrifice and our acceptance of that gift of salvation, God no longer sees us as outcasts and unclean. He sees us as His children—loved, cherished, worthy.

If I had to sum these two tales into one central message, I would have to zero in right smack dab in the middle of the story at the point where the woman had just been healed, and Jairus is at his wit's end with impatience. Though the Bible does not record these words, I have no doubt that Jairus was thinking, "Please, Lord, hurry up. I must save my daughter!" What the ruler didn't realize, however, was that Jesus was busy saving a daughter of His own. Had Jairus spoken his words aloud, I'd like to think that Jesus would have responded something like this: "Yes, Jairus. I know. I know how much you care for your daughter. I know how much you want her healing. I understand your urgency to help her. But, Jairus, just as you love your daughter, so do I love this woman, my daughter. I care for her as you care for your child and am eager for her healing. I have the chance to heal her, and I love her enough to reward her faith."

Two unnamed characters. One, a woman with a twelve-year illness. The other, a girl of twelve years. One outcast and ridiculed. The other loved and cherished. Both healed by a loving Savior. And both of their stories recorded so that we would have an ever-present reminder that Jesus loves and cares for us no matter who we are or what we've done. His healing power is available to all and extends far beyond physical boundaries. He can heal. He can save. He can change our lives in ways that we may never comprehend. The offer is there. All we need to do is reach out and touch Him.

Chapter Six:

HELLO, MY NAME IS _____

And it came to pass, as he went to Jerusalem, that he passed through the midst of Samaria and Galilee. And as he entered into a certain village, there met him ten men that were lepers, which stood afar off: And they lifted up their voices, and said, Jesus, Master, have mercy on us. And when he saw them, he said unto them, Go shew yourselves unto the priests. And it came to pass, that, as they went, they were cleansed. And one of them, when he saw that he was healed, turned back, and with a loud voice glorified God, And fell down on his face at his feet, giving him thanks: and he was a Samaritan. And Jesus answering said, Were there not ten cleansed? but where are the nine? There are not found that returned to give glory to God, save this stranger. And he said unto him, Arise, go thy way: thy faith hath made thee whole. - Luke 17:11-19

No Labels Required

As I read through this account, I am reminded of a sight I came across a few years back. It was a typical day of running errands, and as usual, I was on the lookout for ideas for my daily devotional blog posts. I was not disappointed.

I spied an old, beat-up truck on the side of the road. A man lay underneath the decrepit vehicle, an array of tools surrounding him on every side. The sight should have made me feel sorry for the man, and it would have had it not been for the single word painted across the back window of the truck. There, spelled out in bold yellow letters for all to see, shone the word, "CLUNKER." I chuckled. "No kidding."

Don't get me wrong. I'm not belittling the fellow for having an old vehicle. Jason's bronco (nicknamed *The Beast)* is almost as old as I am. It is covered by as much rust as paint. It possesses a permanent wink from the time it went up against a fallen pine tree. . . and lost. The battery gave up the ghost long ago. The tires won't hold air. Yes, it could appropriately be labeled as "CLUNKER," but please, don't tell Jason I said so. You'll get me in trouble!

I understand that we have to make do with what we have. Really, I do. I just found it amusing that whoever painted that title on the vehicle felt that it was necessary. Anyone could look at the truck and tell it was a clunker. No label was required.

That's the funny thing about labels. Sometimes, they truly are unnecessary while other times, they're helpful. When buying new clothes, for example, there are two important labels to consider. The first one is the tag that specifies what size the article is. Although, in women's clothing, the sizes are wonky and cannot be relied upon. I have a size 4 dress hanging in my closet beside a size 10 dress that fits me exactly the same. What's up with that?

The other label that, to me, is equally important is the care label. It gives vital information on what kind of material the clothing is made of and how to best launder the garment. As far as I'm concerned, if the label reads, "Dry Clean Only," it's the same as saying, "Don't Buy Me." But maybe that's just me.

So yes, while some labels are helpful, others are unnecessary. And sometimes, they're downright hurtful.

Just ask the alcoholic.

The smoker.

The addict.

The single mom.

The unemployed.

The pessimist.

The ex-con.

The backslider.

The orphan.

Or better yet, take a minute to flip through the pages of the leper's diary.

EXCERPT FROM A LEPER'S DIARY

When I first discovered that I had leprosy, I thought the pain would be the worst of it. But I was wrong. So very wrong. I didn't know it was possible to be so lonely, especially when surrounded by others just like me. There are ten of us here at this leper camp, yet each of us knows the pain of wearing labels. Unclean. Outcast. Monster. Leper.

I used to have labels that brought music to my heart and a smile to my lips. My wife called me, "Sweetie." My children called me, "Dad," My friends called me, "Beaver" because of my skill with wood. Hard worker. Carpenter. Friend. Son. Yes, these were the labels I used to go by. But now, those names sound foreign, like a distant memory. The laughter of my children has faded away. The image of my wife diminishes more with each passing day. It's been so long since I've seen them, since I've heard them, since I've held them.

I've thought, on many occasions, about making my way through the back roads to the village and up to the rear of our house. Just to catch a glimpse. But I've always been too afraid. What if someone saw me? I'd be stoned. What if my family saw me? I'd be ashamed. I don't think I could bear to have them look at me with fear and disgust. I know what a sight I must be. My nose and ears are gone. My skin is infested with blotches and welts and ooze. Bleeding sores cover my hands and feet. Even the effort of putting these words to parchment requires more strength than I fear I have. But I must let my feelings go, or I'll lose my mind.

I heard a story last week as I sat in the bushes by the wayside. Two travelers were talking about a man named Jesus. They said He can do miracles. They said He even healed a leper. And get this, He touched him. Yes, Jesus touched the leper. No wonder the people were talking about it. It's simply unheard of. But, that's what they claimed.

I don't want to say anything to the others. I wouldn't want to get their hopes up. But I am now on a mission. I have determined to sit here by the wayside. Surely, this Jesus fellow will have to come by this way sometime. And when He does, I'm going to ask him to heal me too. If it works, I'll tell my friends. I know they miss their families too.

We're not bad people. We're really not. We don't want to hurt anyone. We don't want to frighten anyone. We don't want much, truth be told. We only want to go home. Is that too much to ask?

MEETING THE MASTER

Obviously, we're not privy to the private lives of the ten lepers. But as I've told you before, I have a rather wild imagination, and sometimes it gets the best of me. Whatever the situation, there can be no doubt that the lepers were discouraged and discontent with their lot in life. So much so that they were willing to take a risk when Jesus passed by their way.

The Bible tells us that they stood afar off, but not so far away that their cries could not be heard. How they recognized Jesus, I cannot say. But there's no doubt they did recognize him. They called him by name. *Jesus, Master, have mercy on us!* While it's intriguing to ponder that fact, it's even more exciting when we realize that Jesus recognized each of them and knew their names as well. If He had chosen to do so, He could have told each man his life's story. But He chose to deal with the situation in a different manner.

His response was two-fold, although the first part is often overlooked. It's tempting to jump right into the action. Our impulse is to skip ahead to Jesus' proclamation, but in doing so, we miss a blessing by missing Jesus' initial reaction. When we read the end of the story first, we miss vital parts of the journey, like the reader who skips to the last chapter of a mystery before reading the rest of the book. Where's the fun in that? They've missed the surprise and the suspense. Why bother reading the book if you're only interested in the ending rather than the entire tale?

Every detail in the Bible is important. Every word has a purpose. Every event has an objective. Every phrase has a point. Jesus' first response to the lepers was the most imperative of all. The Bible says, "When he saw them." He saw them!

Not their disease.

Not their disfigurement.

Not their outward appearance.

He saw them.

He saw into their hearts. He saw their pain. He saw their loneliness. He saw their need.

He didn't look at them in disgust. He didn't ignore them and hurry past, like the priest and the Levite did in the story of the Good Samaritan.

He saw them. And while the exact words are not found in this passage, I believe it's safe to say that He was moved with compassion.

Do you remember the story of ***Beauty and the Beast***? A young prince, cruel and vain, denied kindness to an enchantress. As punishment for his rudeness, the enchantress turned the prince into a hideous beast and declared that he should remain that way until he could learn to love and be loved.

The beast whiled away his days in solitary, determined that he would forever remain a monster, for who could ever love a beast? By chance, he meets a young girl who is bold enough to see beyond his growls and grumbles. Because of her good nature and tender heart, she sees in him what no other could see. She sees his brokenness. His loneliness. His pain. His regret. But more than that, she sees what he could be if someone would simply show him the way.

Her compassion and willingness to see beyond the surface awakened a part of the beast that hadn't been there before. He learned to love. To change. To be better. He learned to think of others more than he thought of himself. And in the end, he became a prince once more.

The lepers were the beasts, and Jesus was Beauty. He not only saw what these men were and what they had been, but He also saw what they could be. They only needed a helping hand.

AREN'T YOU FORGETTING SOMETHING?

Working from home has its advantages. For one, I have much more flexibility in my schedule than I did when I worked a teaching job. Another major benefit is that working from home allows me to multi-task, combining my writing and housekeeping chores. For example, as I type this chapter, dinner is cooking away in the crock pot, the sheets are in the washing machine, and between writing sessions, I can spend a few minutes folding clothes or loading the dishwasher.

The entire process, while often convenient, also has a few drawbacks. For starters, sometimes I get so many things going at once that I never really finish any of them. But worst of all is my tendency to forget things. I put the food in the crock pot but forget to turn it on. I load the dishwasher but don't run it. And for my blue-ribbon achievement, I put clothes in the dryer and walk away. Clothes go in. Fabric softener sheet is added. And then the wet clothes sit until it finally dawns on me (usually hours later) that I never heard the dryer buzzer. The clothes in the washer have been ready to be transferred to the dryer, but the process has to be put on hold until the dryer runs a full cycle—something that should have already been done.

If only my dryer could speak, maybe that would help. Yes, that's what I need. Each time I place the clothes in the dryer and close the door, I need my dryer to speak up in burning bush fashion and ask me, "Aren't you forgetting something?" It would probably freak me out, but at least I would remember to turn it on.

Perhaps, the lepers understood all too well. After Jesus saw them, he uttered a single command: "Go show yourselves to the priest." He didn't touch them as he had done with another leper. He didn't proclaim them healed. He didn't apply a salve or whisper a prayer on their behalf. He merely said, "Go."

As was the custom of the time, if a leper was somehow cured of the disease, he was not allowed to return to the city or to his life until first showing himself to the priest. The priest was instructed in what to look for to determine whether he could proclaim the man healed or clean. Leviticus 14:1-2 says, *And the LORD spake unto Moses, saying, This shall be the law of the leper in the day of his cleansing: He shall be brought unto the priest.* From there, the leper and priest were to take part in a specific sacrifice. When that was completed, then, and only then, could the former leper return to his life. For a leper to enter the city without fulfilling these requirements was to invite death.

These ten men knew this. They knew the penalty for entering the city without healing. And as far as they could tell, they weren't healed. Their sores remained. Their extremities, still absent. Why would Jesus command them to do such a thing? Why wouldn't He simply heal them with the power of His words or the compassion of His touch?

Did they wonder?

Did they ask?

Would you?

Let's face it, following God's commands is not always easy, especially when we don't understand what He's doing. When the way ahead looks dark, the last thing we want to do is plow ahead. We want to see the illuminated path. We long to behold the puzzle box with the vivid illustration of the finished work. We desire to see the blueprints of God's will and way. But to step out blindly, well, that's another story, isn't it?

You need two strong legs to complete a strenuous hike. . .Similarly, in your journey with God, faith is a two-step process. It is both an attitude and an action. You believe God loves you, but you need to love him in return. You know God will speak to you, but you need to listen attentively. You have faith that God will guide you and protect you, but you need to follow him and submit to his care. Whenever you take a step of faith in God, follow it with a step of action.[1]

As a hiker, I know the truth of this comparison. Evidently, the lepers did too. The Bible does not record any doubt in their hearts or questions from their lips. What it does record is their action. Whether it was merely because the Lord had commanded it or because they felt they had nothing left to lose, the ten set out on what was possibly the longest walk of their lives. Each of their footfalls echoed out with this proclamation: *We do not live on explanations; we live on promises.*[2]

WHEN FAITH TAKES ACTION

I would love to know how far they walked before they noticed a change in their health. It could be that they were nearly to the priest before their healing took place, but I tend to think that their healing began as soon as they took that first step of faith. It may not have been evident at that moment, but I believe that's when the healing actually began. Who knows for sure? What is certain is that nothing occurred until they obeyed. These men displayed their faith by their action and their obedience. Many times we miss out on the blessings of God because we are unwilling to do our part. We don't understand God's plan, and in our confusion, we disobey. We're unwilling to take the risk, even when we know a miracle is waiting on the other side. And so, we miss the miracle.

The lepers didn't.

If the disciples were with Jesus that day, which I'm inclined to think they were, they didn't miss the action either. Picture them standing on the road, watching as the lepers headed into the distance. With each step, the bodies of the lepers seemed stronger and straighter. Suddenly, a shout was heard from the hillside followed by a silhouette of leaping figures. The disciples watched the elation of the healed, but did any of them notice the expression on the face of the Healer? I imagine it spoke volumes.

Did He have a big smile, or was He wearing a thin smile that didn't quite reach his eyes? Undoubtedly, He was thrilled to have given these men back their lives, but I have to wonder if He was disappointed at their lack of gratitude (even though He had known what was going to happen before He healed them). If you think about it, that portrays the mercy of God right there. He healed the men even when He knew they would forget all about Him once they had received their healing. How many times has God given us things, knowing His goodness would slip our minds as soon as we had what we wanted? It's a sobering thought, isn't it?

A couple of years ago, I was at the hospital with a friend whose daughter was having major surgery on her head. The surgery was scheduled to last nearly ten hours, and I wanted to be there for the family to offer any support and encouragement I could. Unfortunately, I wasn't in a very encouraging mood. In fact, I was in the midst of a major pity party. The previous couple of weeks had been inundated with one problem after another, the biggest of which was our finances (or lack thereof). Money had been tight, and the financial strain was making me crazy. To top it off, I knew that my husband was taking the day off (without pay) to be with the family during this time. I was glad he was there, but my mind wouldn't stop worrying about how we were going to pay the bills. The anxiety consumed both my thoughts and my energy.

As the minutes dragged on, we all sat in a circle, chatting about a myriad of topics in an attempt to distract ourselves from the ongoing surgery. Our pastor told of a blessing he had just received. I don't remember all the details, but the gist of the story was that someone had walked up to him and placed a wad of money in his hand. It may have been a check. I don't remember. But I do remember that it was a nice amount.

At that moment, I caught a stray thought as it made its way to my heart: *I wish the Lord would do something like that for us.* My mind froze, and I was immediately overcome with guilt. How dare I be so ungrateful! How dare I accuse God of not taking care of me or complain about the way He meets my needs! How dare I be so selfish that I couldn't find it in myself to rejoice with my pastor but rather to feel envious of him!

As I processed these thoughts, the Spirit whispered to my soul, "You need to get rid of the bitterness." I knew He was right. At some point, a seed of bitterness had been planted in my heart, and the seed was growing at a rapid pace. I spent the next several weeks struggling to get control of the pesky weed that had invaded my spirit and wrapped its wiry tentacles around my heart, choking out all the gratitude.

Fortunately, as with the nine lepers, God didn't withhold His blessings even though I had withheld my praise. The day after the child's surgery, I went to the bank to deposit Jason's paycheck. I stood at the counter, filling out the deposit slip, then reached into my wallet to pull out his check. There were two checks. With all the hustle and bustle and rearranging of schedules to be at the hospital that day, I had forgotten to deposit his last paycheck. No wonder things had been so tight! Tears streamed down my cheeks as I filled out the deposit slip and laughed my way to the teller. I'm sure the employees and other patrons thought I had lost my mind, but I knew my mind wasn't lost but rather renewed by the reminder that God is faithful, even when I'm not.

To this day, I cringe when I think of how close I came to being completely overtaken by bitterness. Still, I have to guard against ingratitude. Like the nine, I get so caught up in my delight that I forget to praise the Lord. He is so worthy, and He has done so much for me. The least I can do is to say, "Thank you."

THE SOMETHING THAT NEEDS TO BE SAID

As if on cue, a single form appeared once again on the crest of the hill, growing larger as it approached. The disciples immediately recognized the man as one of the healed lepers. Jesus, of course, already knew who it was. The man who before was silenced by his shame, shouted with a loud voice and praised God. He couldn't keep quiet. Falling down on his knees before Christ, he thanked Him over and over again.

Then, notice the odd phrase Luke inserts in the midst of the scene: *and he was a Samaritan.*

Talk about random. What does that have to do with anything? Upon first impression, one might wonder if Luke was suffering from a bit of ADD. But we know that the Bible is God's inspired Word and that everything in it, no matter how irrelevant it may seem, is important. This phrase is no exception.

The Samaritans were a group of people that were outcasts in many respects. They were despised by the Jews partly because they were a society of half-breeds and partly because they had their own thoughts and ideas about religion and worship. Like lepers, they carried around a stigma of being unclean and unworthy. Yet, God makes a special effort to point out that this man was a Samaritan. Could it be God's way of reminding us not to judge others based on our own rules, standards, or convictions? Or perhaps it is His way of humbling us by pointing out that the "unworthy" man was the only one who was virtuous enough to show his gratitude.

Sometimes we think far too much of ourselves. As Christians, we are commanded to be humble in manner and spirit. We are admonished not to think highly of ourselves. But the truth is, we have a tendency to be so impressed by how much we're doing for God that we fail to thank Him for all He's doing for us. We display our "to-do" lists for God like a badge of honor. We complain about the many hats we wear while secretly reveling in the assumption that if the work is to be done right, we must be the ones to do it. And so we glory in ourselves. Meanwhile, God stands at the end of a lonely road waiting patiently for His children to come back and say, "Thanks."

This Samaritan may have been unworthy in the eyes of the world, but Jesus commended him for both his faith and his gratitude. And more than that, it is my firm belief that this man received more than physical healing that day. I believe he received a spiritual healing as well. Unfortunately, the others missed out on that blessing of blessings because they were too caught up in their healing to give thanks to the Healer. May we not be guilty of the same.

We, too, have been infected with a deadly disease. It's called sin. As leprosy eats away at the extremities, sin eats away at the heart. It banishes us to a dark place of isolation and loneliness. It separates us from God just as leprosy separated those infected from their families. It labels us with unmistakable clarity and carries with it a heavy price—death.

113

Thankfully, the Healer passed by our way. For the lepers, His presence brought physical healing; for those who call on His name, He brings salvation. A chance at a new life. An opportunity to be proclaimed "Clean!" For we, too, have a High Priest, before whom we can stand, and thanks to His sacrifice on the cross and our acceptance of that sacrifice, when God looks at us, He sees clean vessels. There is no mark of the disease of sin. We are no longer unclean, dead in our trespasses and sins. There is no more separation. No more isolation. No more devastation.

Yes, we have much to be thankful for! We were once without hope, but now we have hope in Christ. We were without a home, but now we are seated in heavenly places. We have a loving Father who blesses us time and time again even though we don't deserve it. He longs for our praise. How would it thrill His heart if all His creation would come to Him in thanksgiving and offer Him the praise He deserves? I believe the Psalmist said it best, *Oh that men would praise the LORD for his goodness, and for his wonderful works to the children of men!*[3]

There are not found that returned to give glory to God, save this stranger. (Luke 17:18)

O, Lord, let me be the one to say, "Thank you!"

Section Four:

Miracles

of

Resurrection

Chapter Seven:

WHATCHU TALKIN' 'BOUT, JESUS?

Now a certain man was sick, named Lazarus, of Bethany, the town of Mary and her sister Martha. (It was that Mary which anointed the Lord with ointment, and wiped his feet with her hair, whose brother Lazarus was sick.) Therefore his sisters sent unto him, saying, Lord, behold, he whom thou lovest is sick. When Jesus heard that, he said, This sickness is not unto death, but for the glory of God, that the Son of God might be glorified thereby. Now Jesus loved Martha, and her sister, and Lazarus. When he had heard therefore that he was sick, he abode two days still in the same place where he was. Then after that saith he to his disciples, Let us go into Judaea again. His disciples say unto him, Master, the Jews of late sought to stone thee; and goest thou thither again? Jesus answered, Are there not twelve hours in the day? If any man walk in the day, he stumbleth not, because he seeth the light of this world. But if a man walk in the night, he stumbleth, because there is no light in him. These things said he: and after that he saith unto them, Our friend Lazarus sleepeth; but I go, that I may awake him out of sleep. Then said his disciples, Lord, if he sleep, he shall do well. Howbeit Jesus spake of his death: but they thought that he had spoken of taking of rest in sleep. Then said Jesus unto them plainly, Lazarus is dead. And I am glad for your sakes that I was not there, to the intent ye may believe; nevertheless let us go unto him. Then said Thomas, which is called Didymus, unto his fellowdisciples, Let us also go, that we may die with him. Then when Jesus came, he found that he had lain in the grave four days already. Now Bethany was nigh unto Jerusalem, about fifteen furlongs off: And many of the Jews came to Martha and Mary, to comfort them concerning their brother. Then Martha, as soon as she heard that Jesus was coming, went and met him: but Mary sat still in the house. Then said Martha unto Jesus, Lord, if thou hadst been here, my brother had not died. But I know, that even now, whatsoever thou wilt ask of God, God will give it thee. Jesus saith unto her, Thy brother shall rise again. Martha saith unto him, I know that he shall rise again in the resurrection at the last day. Jesus said unto her, I am the resurrection, and the life: he that believeth in me, though he were dead, yet shall he live: And whosoever liveth and believeth in me shall never die. Believest thou this? She saith unto him, Yea, Lord: I believe that thou art the Christ, the Son of God, which should come into the world. And when she had so said, she went her way, and called Mary her sister secretly, saying, The Master is come, and calleth for thee. As soon as she heard that, she arose quickly, and came unto him. Now Jesus was not yet come into the town, but was in that place where Martha met him. The Jews then which were with her in the house, and comforted her, when they saw Mary, that she rose up hastily and went out, followed her, saying, She goeth unto the grave to weep there. Then when Mary was come where Jesus was, and saw him, she fell down at his feet, saying unto him, Lord, if thou hadst been here, my brother had not died. When Jesus therefore saw her weeping, and the Jews also weeping which came with her, he groaned in the spirit, and was troubled. And said, Where have ye laid him? They said unto him, Lord, come and see. Jesus wept. Then said the Jews, Behold how he loved him! And some of them said, Could not this man, which opened the eyes of the blind, have caused that even this man should not have died? Jesus therefore again groaning in himself cometh to the grave. It was a cave, and a stone lay upon it. Jesus said, Take ye away the stone. Martha, the sister of him that was dead, saith unto him, Lord, by this time he stinketh: for he hath been dead four days. Jesus saith unto her, Said I not unto thee, that, if thou wouldest believe, thou shouldest see the glory of God? Then they took away the stone from the place where the dead was laid. And Jesus lifted up his eyes, and said, Father, I thank thee that thou hast heard me. And I knew that thou hearest me always: but because of the people which stand by I said it, that they may believe that thou hast sent me. And when he thus had spoken, he cried with a loud voice, Lazarus, come forth. And he that was dead came forth, bound hand and foot with graveclothes: and his face was bound about with a napkin. Jesus saith unto them, Loose him, and let him go. Then many of the Jews which came to Mary, and had seen the things which Jesus did, believed on him. - John 11:1-45

Jason and I were supposed to be attending a concert tonight. We've had it on the calendar for months. We've talked about it and made plans. The only thing left to do was to get information on ticket prices.

Last week, I attempted to do that very thing. I pulled up the church's website to find out the information we needed. But something was wrong with the website, and each time I clicked on a tab, I was taken to an error page. "Oh well," I proclaimed after several attempts. "I guess I'll just call them tomorrow."

As usual, tomorrow came and went, and in the busyness of my schedule, I forgot to call until earlier this week. I looked up the number, placed the call and spoke to a very kind lady who informed me that the tickets were free. I was ecstatic. . . temporarily. On the heels of her exciting announcement, she informed me that, because of safety codes, the Fire Marshal had set a limit on how many tickets they could give away. Unfortunately, they had reached that limit over a week ago.

"Is there any way to get in?" I pleaded.

"I'm sorry," she replied. "Not without a ticket."

I was nearly in tears as I hung up the phone. How was I going to tell Jason? He was really looking forward to this concert. I was really looking forward to it. After the past few weeks we've had, we NEEDED this concert. I was disappointed beyond belief. Everything had been set. Everything seemed to be falling into place. Yet, because we waited too long to contact the church, we'll be spending our evening in an entirely different way. One week too late! Just one measly week!

If ever anyone understood the disappointment that results from tardiness, it was Mary and Martha. These two sisters, along with their brother, Lazarus, pop in and out of several stories throughout the gospels. Besides the disciples, no other specific family or friend is mentioned quite as often as this trio. This repetition, if nothing else, serves to prove the relationship between Jesus and the siblings. There was love, no doubt about it. Mary and Martha knew it, for in their request to Jesus, they said, *He whom thou lovest is sick.* John was aware of the closeness for in verse five he declares, *Now Jesus loved Martha, and her sister, and Lazarus.* Yes, the relationship was unmistakable, which leads many to question why Lazarus was sick at all. In this day of the "health and wealth" mentality, it's difficult for some to understand why one so dear to Jesus would be overcome with so great an illness.

Dr. David Jeremiah says, *When we go through hard times, everybody on the street has an opinion about why it is happening, where we should go for help, and what's going on. Isn't it confusing?[1]*

It certainly was for Dr. Harold B. Sightler, former pastor of Tabernacle Baptist Church in Greenville, SC.

While he was away preaching at a revival meeting, Sightler's wife and two daughters were struck by a drunk driver. His wife was taken to the hospital for treatment for multiple injuries including a brain contusion, a concussion, a broken jaw and the loss of several teeth. His daughter, Elizabeth, though bumped and bruised, was relatively unharmed. His other daughter, Carolyn, however, died of her injuries before Dr. Sightler arrived at the hospital.

In the following days, many friends and fellow pastors phoned, wrote, or stopped by to offer condolences and encouragement. Some, like Horace Stansbury, spoke words that uplifted the downcast eyes and helped mend the broken hearts. Stansbury, who had also lost a young child, told Sightler, "Son, I came down to tell you that I was glad God had a preacher in South Carolina that he wasn't afraid to turn the devil loose on. You can't go any deeper; your next move is up."

Some had comments that weren't so helpful. Despite the family's distress, one man dared to ask the faithful preacher, "So, what have you done to deserve such tragedy? What sin in your life is God trying to address? Just what is God trying to say to you?" I don't know how Sightler responded to such an impertinent question, but I can guarantee you it was nicer than the way I would have. What right did he have to assume that their suffering was a result of sin? His question only served to illustrate his ignorance.

It's time we settle this matter once and for all. When bad things happen, it does not mean that God does not care. It is not an indication that our prayers have gone unheard or unanswered. It is not necessarily a symptom of an unhealthy relationship with God or with others. It's just a part of life. In John 16:33, Jesus said, *In the world ye shall have tribulation.* It's going to happen. Life is not always going to be a bed of roses, even for the Christian. The benefit for the children of God is that we have Someone walking through the fire with us, but we must understand that the Bible never indicates that we won't ever feel the heat. On the contrary, it compares us to clay in the Potter's hands. Clay that must be molded, have pressure applied, then spend some time on the wheel before being sent to the fire where it can harden, making the clay stable and fit for use. Yes, we'll go through the fire, but catch that: through. We're not there to stay. It's only temporary. It will pass.

THE PAIN OF UNMET EXPECTATIONS

When tragedy struck, Mary and Martha wasted no time. They knew where to turn. They had a Friend to call on. They knew what He could do. They had seen Him prove His power. I believe there was no doubt in either of their minds what Jesus would do. With unwavering faith, they sent a servant to inform Jesus that Lazarus was sick, knowing that Jesus would rush to his side and heal him as He had done for so many others. But once again, Christ reminds us that His ways are not our ways. We may never understand the reason for Lazarus' sickness, but we can't escape the reason for his death. Jesus makes it quite clear.

I can only imagine what must have been going on in the mind of the servant who brought the news to Jesus, for Christ's response was indeed a mysterious one. *This sickness is not unto death, but for the glory of God, that the Son of God might be glorified thereby.* If I were the servant, I would have understood Jesus to have said, "Don't worry. Lazarus won't die. Everything is going to be fine." In fact, for all we know, that could be exactly how the servant interpreted Jesus' response. The Bible doesn't say, but I would assume, the servant rushed back with the good news. I imagine he barged into the house and stood before the two sorrowful sisters. "Jesus said

123

not to worry because Lazarus is going to be just fine." Only after he had exploded with the news did he notice the pale, still form on the bed. Lazarus was already dead.

I think we all understand the heartache that comes when God doesn't work the way we want Him to. We ask for sunshine, and He sends rain. We plead for gain, and He sends only loss. We request peace, yet find ourselves in the midst of turmoil. It seems so unfair. It seems so unloving. How can our Heavenly Father look down on our plight and not heed our requests? According to Christian author, Max Lucado, *When God doesn't do what we want, it's not easy. Never has been. Never will be. But faith is the conviction that God knows more than we do about this life and he will get us through it. Remember, disappointment is caused by unmet expectations. Disappointment is cured by revamped expectations.* [2]

It's so easy to get wrapped up in this life to the point that we don't even realize that we have no idea what's truly best for us. We know what seems best. We know what seems right and good. We know how we want things to turn out. But we have no clue because we can't see the entire picture. We can't fathom how the decisions of today will affect all our tomorrows. Yet, so often, we still find it easier to trust in ourselves than in God, who does see the whole picture. He's holding the top of the puzzle box while we're left staring at a handful of individual pieces. We can't see where the pieces go because we don't know what the picture is supposed to look like. God knows. God cares. God has a plan, but sometimes, for that plan to come about, we must first face the undesirable. Mary and Martha certainly did.

For all the sisters knew, Jesus had forsaken them. He said He was coming, but He never showed up. They had counted on Him, and He had let them down. They had no idea that God had a much bigger and better plan in place. They only knew their disappointment.

CONFUSING CONCEPTS

A few days later, Jesus told his disciples, "Okay, let's go see Lazarus now."

"Now?" they questioned. "You want to go now? But why? You didn't want to go two days ago."

Aren't you glad God is not offended by our questions? I don't know about you, but I've asked some doozies in my time. Where? When? Why? How? Yet none of them have caused God to turn away in anger or disgust. He understands that our questions are merely an outpouring of our hearts, and He welcomes them as such. However, when our questions turn to demands for answers, then we're crossing a line. We go from pleading to accusing, and that is unacceptable. *It is not wrong to ask questions of God, but it is wrong to question God. The prophet Habakkuk asked God many questions, and God answered him; but his attitude was one of submissive concern and not rebellious complaint.*[3]

Yes, we can ask, but keep in mind we don't need to know the why and the how. All we need to know is that God is faithful and that He works all things for our good. Evidently, the disciples hadn't quite grasped that concept either.

Amidst their many inquiries, they pointed out that the last time Jesus was in Judea, the Jews had sought to stone Him. To their finite minds, it didn't make sense for Jesus to risk His life for a friend that He claimed was going to be fine. Try as we might, we will never understand the ways of God. They don't make sense to us. And to prove my point, look at what Jesus said next.

Lazarus is dead. And I am glad for your sakes that I was not there, to the intent ye may believe; nevertheless let us go unto him. Does that verse strike anyone else as odd? The first two phrases just don't seem to go together. "Lazarus is dead, and I'm glad I was not there." Talk about sounding heartless. Good grief!

My grandmother is the most blunt and plain-spoken person I know. She says what she means and means what she says. She doesn't pull any punches. If she thinks you need to pull your pants up, she'll tell you. If she thinks your hair resembles that of an unemployed clown, she'll tell you that too. It's not that she's mean. She's just painstakingly honest. . . sometimes to the point of embarrassing those who are around her.

But I must admit, in this case, Jesus makes my grandmother look reserved. "Lazarus is dead, and I'm glad I was not there." If the disciples weren't confused before, they were now. That is, if they do like the rest of us and only hear part of what the Lord says. Could it be that the bluntness of the statement caught them off guard to where they missed the part of why Jesus was glad?

For their sakes.

So that they might believe.

Jesus was glad for another opportunity to prove Himself to the disciples.

It was love that compelled Him to go. Love for His disciples. Love for Mary, Martha, and Lazarus. Love for the unnamed mourners He would find at the tomb. Yes, His love compelled Him to go, just as it compelled Him to come to earth for the sake of raising us from our death in trespasses and sins. He didn't have to come. He could have let us remain in our sins just as He could have let Lazarus remain in the grave. He didn't have to leave the splendor of Heaven. But He loved us too much to stay away. And so He came, destined to be the sacrifice for our sins so that we could be raised in newness of life. Oh, what love!

A MESSAGE FOR THE MOURNERS

When the entourage finally arrived, they discovered that Lazarus had been in the grave for four days. Four days! For four days, Mary and Martha had been wondering why Jesus didn't come. For four days, friends and neighbors had been whispering about the Friend who had let them down. For four days, doubt and discouragement ate away at the hearts of the two sisters. No doubt, those four days seemed like an eternity.

Four days is a long time to wait for a resurrection, especially when you feel that all hope is gone. Figuratively, you may be living in those dark 96 hours before dawn, wondering if the 5,760 minutes will ever end. Each of the 345,000 seconds that make up your waiting seems to hold its breath interminably, like my malfunctioning metronome, leaving you suspended between faith and doubt. Wondering if the dissonant chord hanging over your life will ever be resolved. Four days is a long time to wait. I know. I've endured the incessant length myself. But believe me, none of it is wasted time.[4]

As difficult as it can be, we must learn to accept God's timing. Yes, His ears are always open to our cries, but that does not mean that He is at our beck and call. We must trust in His perfect plan, learning to live on His promises, content with His timetable.

Martha, despite her attitude problem in Luke 10, seems to be grasping the importance of the rebuke Jesus had given her. When she heard that Jesus was finally coming, she couldn't bear to wait any longer. The Bible says that she ran out to meet him, and the first words out of her mouth were the words I'm sure any of us would have uttered in her situation: "Lord, if You had been here, Lazarus would still be alive." Martha had faith in Christ's power but not in His timing. Her grief was the first to speak, followed quickly by her faith: *But I know, that even now, whatsoever thou wilt ask of God, God will give it thee.* I'm not sure exactly what Martha had in mind, but I don't think it was the resurrection of Lazarus because when Jesus told her that Lazarus would be raised, she replied, *I know that he shall rise again in the resurrection at the last day.* In other words, "I know he'll be raised again in the end when we're all raised from the dead." She knew Jesus *could* do something, but I'm not sure she fully believed He *would* do something.

Jesus then spoke some of the most beautiful and powerful words in all the Bible, *I am the resurrection, and the life: he that believeth in me, though he were dead, yet shall he live: And whosoever liveth and believeth in me shall never die.* That is the reason the Bible says, *But I would not have you to be ignorant, brethren, concerning them which are asleep, that ye sorrow not, even as others which have no hope. For if we believe that Jesus died and rose again, even so them also which sleep in Jesus will God bring with him.* [5]

When a fellow Christian dies, it is a sorrowful time, but we can rest in the hope that we will see that loved one again. Because of Jesus, we have a hope. Martha somewhat understood that hope and ran off to tell Mary that Jesus had finally come.

MISSING MARY

It speaks volumes to me that Mary didn't run out with Martha when word first came that Jesus was coming. Strange, don't you think? After all, this was the woman who sat at the feet of Jesus. This was the woman who washed His feet with her hair and anointed Him with oil. This was Mary, who loved Jesus and had shown Him such devotion. Why didn't she make haste to greet Him? Why wasn't she running into His arms? Could it be that she was so overcome by grief that she just couldn't face Him?

For those of you who are not pet lovers, you may want to skip this part because you just won't understand. I have two dogs, but they are not treated like pets. They are like my children. They act like children, whining when they don't get their way, seeking love and attention, basking in the praise of their mommy and daddy, etc. I love my dogs as if they were my children. They are a part of my family, and in a sense, a part of myself.

A few years back, my husband and I noticed a lump around the mouth of our Chow mix, Tessa. She was a precious dog of ten years. We had raised her since she was eight weeks old. She and I had a special bond that had formed the day we adopted her from the Animal Shelter, and she had laid her fluffy little head on my shoulder. It was love at first sight, and even though we were looking for a much smaller dog, I had made up my mind. Jason really didn't have a say in the matter. Sorry, sweetie!

After noticing the growth, we continued to watch to see if any changes occurred. My initial thought was that she had a bad tooth that was causing her gums to swell. I wish it had been that simple. When we determined that the lump wasn't getting any better, we took her to the vet. Because of the problem being in her mouth, they had to put her to sleep long enough to examine inside the mouth to discover the problem. A few hours later, we received the call informing us that Tessa had severe cancer. It was in her mouth, down her throat and possibly scattered throughout the rest of her body. We had to make a decision about what to do. We couldn't afford cancer treatments, and frankly, I didn't want to put Tessa through that ordeal. We decided to bring her home and make her as comfortable as possible. As long as she was enjoying life, we weren't going to take it from her.

Unfortunately, she went downhill very rapidly. By the end of the week, she had lost control of her bladder, she couldn't eat and overall seemed very lethargic. After many tears, my husband and I both decided that it wasn't fair to make her suffer any longer, and we called the vet to set up a time to put Tessa down.

It was the hardest decision I've ever had to make, but it was nothing compared to the months of mourning to follow.

I couldn't go with Tessa to the vet. I knew I would be a basket-case, and I didn't want to scare her with my hysteria. My husband bravely stepped up and offered to take her. It's one of the few times I've ever seen him cry. The entire time he was gone, I sat on the bed, my arms wrapped around our beagle, Tippy, and sobbed. I couldn't imagine life without my baby, Tessa.

I honestly don't remember what we did Friday night or all day Saturday. It's such a blur. I remember crying, and I remember trying to keep my mind off the loss. But I don't remember the specific events. I remember Sunday though. Jason and I were scheduled to take part in a special worship service for a photographer's convention of which his parents were members. Jason was supposed to bring a short devotion. I was supposed to sing and play the piano. After that, we had planned to drive back to our church for our Homecoming Sunday.

I felt like a zombie. I didn't want to go anywhere. I didn't want to see anyone. I didn't want to talk to anyone. I just wanted to cry. The last thing I wanted to do was to be around other people. But we both felt obligated to go, and so we went. I thought I was fairly composed that morning although I had already determined that there was no way I could sing. Jason's dad met us at the door and embraced me in a comforting hug. I broke down. I managed to compose myself again and made it through the service. We finished up and made our way to our church.

Many of the people there were aware of what we had faced that week and came up to me to offer their condolences. Several of the ladies offered hugs of encouragement. I fell apart every time. I appreciated their kindness. I really did. But I didn't want to make a scene, and I just couldn't seem to hold myself together. It seemed like every word or action of sympathy brought a fresh renewal of my grief. It was more than I could stand. Even now, tears are streaming down my face. I've heard it said that time heals all wounds, but whoever composed that quote obviously never lost a loved one. Time does not heal all wounds. It makes the wounds easier to accept and sometimes to understand, but it does not bring healing. *Time does not cause healing; it is simply the context for God's healing ingredients to interact with your situation. All the other elements that God uses to make a way are still necessary...Time alone is rarely enough.* [6]

Recalling those events, I have to wonder if it was pain that held Mary back. Perhaps she was at a place like I was where she just couldn't face another sympathetic smile or hug. I don't know, but when Martha returned for her, we see that Mary didn't waste any time. She ran to Jesus and uttered the exact same words that Martha had spoken. But notice, she left off the last part. She made no proclamation of faith.

But I love Jesus' reaction. *He groaned in the spirit and was troubled.* Jesus was troubled because Mary was troubled. He was hurting because she was hurting. He understood her grief, discouragement, and confusion. He understood her tears. Did you know God keeps our tears in a bottle? *Thou tellest my wanderings:*

put thou my tears into thy bottle: are they not in thy book?[7]

Some of us may have bigger bottles than others. Who am I kidding? Mine must be a barrel! The point is that not one tear goes unnoticed. No matter what you may be going through, Jesus understands. Marshall Hall and Benji Gaither put this thought into words when they wrote the song, "When I Cry." The chorus states, "When I cry, You cry. When I hurt, You hurt. When I've lost someone, it takes a piece of You too. And when I fall on my face, You fill me with grace 'cause nothing breaks Your heart, or tears You apart like when I cry."[8]

Isn't it a blessing to know we have such a compassionate Savior?

And as if His groaning spirit wasn't enough, John goes on to tell us that Jesus wept. There's no record that Jesus wept when John the Baptist, his cousin, was killed. Jesus Himself said that there was no greater man born of women than John the Baptist, yet there's no mention of Jesus shedding tears at his murder. Why the tears now? Didn't Jesus say He was glad that He hadn't been there just a few verses earlier? Why the sudden sadness?

I have a few theories, the first being the one I already mentioned about Jesus sorrowing over the sorrow of His friends. I'm one of those people who can't see someone else crying without joining in. My husband says I'm tenderhearted. Whatever the case, if you cry around me, be warned that I will cry too. Jesus was certainly tenderhearted, so perhaps His tears were sorrow for Mary and Martha because of their having to suffer so much pain.

Perhaps He was mourning the unbelief of the people—His friends and disciples included. He had done so much for them. He had performed miracles. He had explained His plan and purpose. He had proven to them that nothing was beyond Him. No task was too great. No foe too powerful. Yet still, they didn't believe. Yes, it could be that His tears were those of frustration for a crowd that just didn't get it.

It could also be that Jesus wept for Lazarus. Yes, I know Lazarus was dead, but we have to remember he was only dead in the flesh. His spirit was alive and well in Paradise. The Bible says that to be absent from the body is to be present with the Lord. Lazarus was absent from his body, so it's safe to assume He was present with the Lord. He was in a better place. He was healed. His body no longer ached. He was free from the burden of time, of age, of physical restraints. Lazarus was much better off where he was. I wonder how he felt about being called back to "the real world." Can you imagine spending four days in absolute bliss and then having to return to the nasty now and now? Jesus knew what Lazarus would have to give up when he was called back. Isn't it possible his tears were for Lazarus?

Or maybe Dr. Harold B. Sightler is on the right track. *Jesus wept because of death that had broken the heart of His friends. He wept because of sin. Sin always brings death. He wept because of the souls of men that sometimes die without God and without hope. Now, Lazarus was a believer and was ready to meet God in death, but our Lord weeps over the potential millions who die without God. He is a compassionate Savior!*[9]

A LITTLE HELP, PLEASE

Picture the tear-stained face of Jesus as He stood at the tomb of Lazarus and commanded for the stone to be rolled away. The stone symbolizes some different obstacles. In the case of Lazarus, the stone was the obstacle separating him from life and death. For the bystanders, it was the obstacle separating them from doubt and faith. For us, it serves as a picture of the sin that separates us from our Savior. Fortunately, God is skilled at removing obstacles. When He has a plan, nothing can thwart it. And sometimes He even lets us help!

Jesus didn't need the people to roll back the stone. He could have done it Himself. Wouldn't that have been impressive? One man moving a massive gravestone. Surely, that would have gotten the people's attention. For that matter, He could have spoken to the stone and caused it to roll away of its own accord. Now that's proof of power, right? But no, He allowed the people to take part. What a blessing that God can and will allow us to be a part of the miracles He's working in our lives and in the lives of others.

I remember back when I taught kindergarten how I would enlist the students' help in various tasks around the classroom. While some teachers mocked my audacity to enforce "child slave labor," others understood that, to a five-year-old, helping the teacher was a delight, not a duty. If I needed someone to crawl around on the floor and pick up the paper, there was never a shortage of volunteers. Whatever the task, whether it be removing staples from a bulletin board, arranging papers or wiping down countertops, the students were always willing to take part. After all, what child wouldn't want the opportunity to get out of his/her seat and walk around the room or crawl across the floor?

You know what else? When the day was done, and we stood in car line, I was always amazed at the first thing out of the students' mouths. When the car doors opened, did they tell their mom or dad about recess or the new country they had learned about that day or about the birthday cake they had at lunch? Not typically. On the contrary, on most occasions, the first sentence out of their mouths was, "I got to help Mrs. Rongione today. Guess what job I did."

They loved it! They couldn't get enough of it. And because I understood their joy, I made an effort to get all the students involved and to mix up the chores as much as possible so that every child could have the opportunity to do the job he/she wanted to do. Sure, I could have done the chores myself. In fact, sometimes I had to go back and do them anyway because they were done by a five-year-old according to a five-year-old's standards. But that's okay. I didn't mind because I knew I was instilling in them good work habits and good attitudes, but more importantly, I was giving them an opportunity to "help the teacher."

God does the same for us. Sure, He could do the work Himself, and He could do a far better job than we're even capable of. But that's not what matters to Him. What matters to Him is that we have the chance to "help the Teacher," for He knows we get as excited about it as my five-year-olds did.

A TIME FOR BEING SET FREE

John did such an excellent job setting the scene here. The story has been exciting with all the proper twists and turns. We're all on the edge of our seats. Let's get to the good part, right? Let's see the miracle. We will, I assure you, but there's more to be gained in Jesus' next act.

Then they took away the stone from the place where the dead was laid. And Jesus lifted up his eyes, and said, Father, I thank thee that thou hast heard me. And I knew that thou hearest me always: but because of the people which stand by I said it, that they may believe that thou hast sent me. (John 11:41-42)

The fact that Jesus is talking to God is, in itself, mind-boggling. How can Jesus talk to God when He is God? Don't think on it too long; you'll give yourself a headache. If you're going to meditate on something, how about this: Jesus thanked God before the miracle took place. He thanked God for hearing Him and basically for meeting His need before He even asked it. I'm bad to forget to thank God for things after the fact, let alone before, but we should. Anytime we ask for something, we should follow that request with a prayer of thanksgiving for God answering the prayer He has yet to answer. *Be careful for nothing; but in every thing by prayer and supplication with thanksgiving let your requests be made known unto God.*[10]

Did you catch that? Prayer and supplication WITH thanksgiving. They go hand in hand. We should never initiate one without the other. If Jesus thought it was important to thank God, shouldn't we? In fact, didn't we learn that lesson from the lepers?

THE GRAND FINALE

And when he thus had spoken, he cried with a loud voice, Lazarus, come forth. And he that was dead came forth. (John 11:43-44a)

Now, I've heard it said that if Jesus hadn't called Lazarus by name, the entire graveyard would have risen to life. If you believe that, that's fine, but I think that's putting a mighty big limit on a limitless God. Seriously, Jesus didn't have to speak at all. He could have called Lazarus forth without uttering a word. It was His power that raised Lazarus from the dead, and I believe Jesus knew how to use His power well enough that He understood what it took to raise one man from the dead as opposed to the entire graveyard. Besides which, what are the chances that Lazarus, the brother of Mary and Martha, was the only Lazarus in that graveyard? It was a popular enough name. By saying that the entire graveyard would have come forth, to me, is implying that Jesus had no control over His power. And that just isn't so. When He calmed the storm on the sea of Galilee, He didn't specify, "Wind and waves, be still." No, He said, "Peace, be still." So does that mean the fish stopped swimming and the birds stopped flying? Of course not. We have a bad habit of putting our mighty, big God in a little, tiny box. That being said, I think Jesus' use of Lazarus' name can serve as a reminder of three things: (1) We serve a personal Savior, (2) He knows our names, and (3) We should be specific when we make requests of

Him. God likes to hear the specifics, even though He already understands the circumstance better than we do.

Poor Lazarus! Bound up like a mummy, hopping to the entrance of the cave. At least, I would assume he hopped. From all the pictures I've seen of corpses wrapped for burial, I can't see how he would have walked, and the Bible clearly says "he came forth." Once again, however, this gives the people an opportunity to take part in the miracle. Can you imagine the conversations that took place in the weeks that followed?

"Hey, did you hear that story about Lazarus?"

"You mean the one Jesus raised from the dead?"

"Yeah, wouldn't you have loved to have been there?"

"I was there. In fact, I was one of the guys who helped move the stone. Shoo! You can't imagine the smell coming from that cave."

"Seriously? You were there? You got to open the tomb?"

"That's nothing," another man chimes in, "I got to remove his graveclothes."

Well, there's a tale you don't hear every day. That's for sure, but I imagine it was the talk of the town for quite a while. Jesus certainly succeeded in creating a stir. Thankfully, that wasn't all He accomplished. In fact, He achieved the very thing He had sought to do. At the end of the story, everything finally makes sense. The disregard. The delay. All the questions and mysteries can be laid to rest in verse 45: *Then many of the Jews which came to Mary, and had seen the things which Jesus did, believed on him.* Jesus was on a mission for souls.

I guarantee that if we could talk with Mary and Martha today, we would find out some interesting things. But above all, I believe they would tell us that it was worth all the heartache and pain, all the doubt and confusion to see those souls saved. It was a price they would willingly pay again.

What about us? Can we say the same? In the midst of confusion, when God delays, are we willing to trust that He has a greater plan and that He will bring that plan about in His own time? Are we willing to suffer temporary heartache and grief if it means seeing souls saved? Do we trust God enough to allow Him to use circumstances in our own lives to be the tools that bring others to Him? And how about Lazarus? He left splendor to heed the call of Christ. Are we even willing to step out of our comfort zones? Are we listening for His call?

In 890 A.D., the tomb of Lazarus (his final resting place) was discovered. The inscription on the sarcophagus read, "Lazarus. . .friend of Christ." What a testimony! I pray that as much can be said about me, but even more so, I long to hear God Himself call me a friend. In my mind, there is no greater praise!

Chapter Eight:

TALES FROM THE CRYPT

For reasons that will soon be evident, this chapter is going to be a little different than the others (and probably a bit longer). Why? Well, to put it simply, this chapter is about the miracle of all miracles in the New Testament. This is the miracle on which our Christian lives are based, for you see, for us to be saved, a holy sacrifice had to be made. We know that Jesus was that sacrifice. But it wasn't enough for Jesus to die; He also had to rise again. And that glorious fulfillment of prophecy is what we'll be discussing in this chapter.

As I've previously stated, the resurrection of Christ is mentioned in all four of the gospels, and rightly so. Not only that, there are so many details surrounding the miraculous act, that I feel it would be best to split this chapter into sections based on the cast of characters involved in the resurrection story. So, without further ado, let's meet some people who have quite a story to share.

THE TWO ON THE ROAD TO EMMAUS

And, behold, two of them went that same day to a village called Emmaus, which was from Jerusalem about threescore furlongs. And they talked together of all these things which had happened. And it came to pass, that, while they communed together and reasoned, Jesus himself drew near, and went with them. But their eyes were holden that they should not know him. And he said unto them, What manner of communications are these that ye have one to another, as ye walk, and are sad? And the one of them, whose name was Cleopas, answering said unto him, Art thou only a stranger in Jerusalem, and hast not known the things which are come to pass there in these days? And he said unto them, What things? And they said unto him, Concerning Jesus of Nazareth, which was a prophet mighty in deed and word before God and all the people: And how the chief priests and our rulers delivered him to be condemned to death, and have crucified him. But we trusted that it had been he which should have redeemed Israel: and beside all this, to day is the third day since these things were done. Yea, and certain women also of our company made us astonished, which were early at the sepulchre; And when they found not his body, they came, saying, that they had also seen a vision of angels, which said that he was alive. And certain of them which were with us went to the sepulchre, and found it even so as the women had said: but him they saw not. Then he said unto them, O fools, and slow of heart to believe all that the prophets have spoken: Ought not Christ to have suffered these things, and to enter into his glory? And beginning at Moses and all the prophets, he expounded unto them in all the scriptures the things concerning himself. And they drew nigh unto the village, whither they went: and he made as though he would have gone further. But they constrained him, saying, Abide with us: for it is toward evening, and the day is far spent. And he went in to tarry with them. And it came to pass, as he sat at meat with them, he took bread, and blessed it, and brake, and gave to them. And their eyes were opened,

*and they knew him; and he vanished out of their sight.
And they said one to another, Did not our heart burn
within us, while he talked with us by the way, and while
he opened to us the scriptures? And they rose up the
same hour, and returned to Jerusalem, and found the
eleven gathered together, and them that were with them,
Saying, The Lord is risen indeed, and hath appeared to
Simon. And they told what things were done in the way,
and how he was known of them in breaking of bread.
(Luke 24:13-35)*

If ever there were a scene of hopelessness and
despair, the first few verses of this text exhibit one. Here
we see two of Jesus' followers journeying home after the
resurrection. Like so many others, they had placed all
their hope in Christ, and now He was gone.

It's difficult to say exactly who these people
were. Verse 18 tells us clearly that one of them was
called "Cleopas." As for the identity of the other, there's
no concrete evidence one way or another, but I'll tell you
my theory. (If you haven't figured it out by now, I have a
lot of theories.) I think the other may have been Mary,
the sister of Mary, the mother of Jesus (i.e. Jesus' aunt).
My reasoning behind this suggestion can be found in
John 19:25 — *Now there stood by the cross of Jesus his
mother, and his mother's sister, Mary the wife of
Cleophas, and Mary Magdalene.* It's not at all
uncommon to see names spelled two or three different
ways throughout Scripture. It isn't a contradiction but
rather differences in who was writing at the time and
from what culture they were raised. "Savior" and
"Saviour" are both correct spellings, and the two words
mean exactly the same thing. One is what we refer to as

143

old English. Simply put, spellings change. So, I truly believe this other traveler could be Mary, the wife of Cleopas and sister of Mary and aunt of Jesus. (Please note, this is only my opinion— take it or leave it.)

To be completely honest, however, what's more important than who these people were is where they were going. They were walking the seven-mile journey from Jerusalem to Emmaus. They were walking away from God's promises. They were giving up. The couple had high expectations, an idea of how things were supposed to work out, but when things didn't go according to their outline, rather than trusting in the One who had spelled out *His* plan time and again, they walked away. Back to their old ways. Back to their state of hopelessness. I wish I could say that I had no idea what that's like, but I fear I can't. Sadly, I've walked in their shoes. Tired. Discouraged. Defeated. *Why didn't things work out? I was so sure this was the answer.* In fact, the two on Emmaus were probably asking the same thing. The Bible says "they communed together and reasoned." In other words, they were talking it out and trying to figure out where they went wrong.

The saddest part about this scene is that it was completely unnecessary. There was no cause for their doubt and disappointment.

Yea, and certain women also of our company made us astonished, which were early at the sepulchre; And when they found not his body, they came, saying, that they had also seen a vision of angels, which said that he was alive. And certain of them which were with us went to the sepulchre, and found it even so as the women had said: but him they saw not. (Luke 24:22-24)

144

Is it just me, or does that sound like good news? Cleopas himself told the Stranger, "Yeah, some friends of ours visited the tomb, but when they got there Jesus was gone. There was an angel there, they said, who told them that Jesus was alive. Sure enough, some other friends went to the tomb, and everything was just like the women had said." Well, that's great, Cleopas! What's the matter with you? That means Jesus is alive. That means He kept His promise. That means He conquered death. That means He can be trusted. That means He is Who you thought He was. This is fantastic! You should be dancing at the tomb instead of moping down the road.

Not only did the couple not believe what they heard about Jesus being alive, but they were also so blinded by their discouragement that they didn't recognize the Man walking with them. A powerful point to drive home here is this—just because God is walking with us doesn't mean we're walking with Him. Jesus was there with them, and they didn't even notice. They were so focused on their foiled plans and dashed dreams that they failed to see the Answer to all of their problems standing before them. But that was about to change.

As Jesus joined the couple on the road, He couldn't help but notice their somber mood and hushed tones. *And he said unto them, What manner of communications are these that ye have one to another, as ye walk, and are sad?* Isn't it comforting to know that even when our emotions lie to us and blind us from the truth, Jesus still cares? He was genuinely concerned that His followers were so distraught. Cleopas was quick to answer, and from the sounds of it, he was a bit harsh. "What? Are you a stranger here that you haven't heard?

145

Everybody's talking about the things that have happened the past few days."

Jesus simply smiled an innocent smile and asked, "What things?" If that's not proof that the Lord has a sense of humor, I don't know what is. After all He had been through the past few days, all He chose to say was, "What things?" My pastor always reminds us that Jesus doesn't ask questions to learn something; He asks questions to teach something. I believe that's the case in this situation too. Sometimes if we go back and review what we know, we'll often find the solution that was eluding us before. Unfortunately, even after Cleopas stated the truth with his own mouth, he didn't get it. Do you know when Cleopas finally started to see the truth? When he stopped talking and started listening. Do you know when we'll see the truth? When we learn to do the same.

Then he said unto them, O fools, and slow of heart to believe all that the prophets have spoken: Ought not Christ to have suffered these things, and to enter into his glory? And beginning at Moses and all the prophets, he expounded unto them in all the scriptures the things concerning himself. (Luke 24:25-27)

Like a frustrated teacher, Jesus looked at his bleary-eyed students and said, "Okay, let's start back at the beginning." And that's exactly what he did. He went back to the beginning of the Bible and showed them God's plan. Jesus was to come and be born of a woman. He would die a horrible death on the cross. He would remain in the tomb for three days and three nights, but then He would arise again. This was God's plan! It had been spelled out in black and white for thousands of years. But just to make sure the two weary travelers really understood, he offered more evidence.

And he went in to tarry with them. And it came to pass, as he sat at meat with them, he took bread, and blessed it, and brake, and gave to them. And their eyes were opened, and they knew him; and he vanished out of their sight. And they said one to another, Did not our heart burn within us, while he talked with us by the way, and while he opened to us the scriptures? (Luke 24:29b-32)

Sometimes we need to be still for things to become clear. I love to take pictures, and through our various hiking excursions, I've had the opportunity to capture some lovely images. My problem, though, is that nine times out of ten, my pictures end up blurry. And the main cause of blurry images is that either the camera or the object of the photograph is not still. (In my case, it's usually the camera because I can't seem to keep my hands from shaking. I guess I need to invest in a tripod, huh?) The point is that time and time again, I miss out on priceless photo opportunities because I just can't be still. How often is that the case in our lives? How many times do we miss out on God's blessings because we're always on the go? How often is our view of life blurry because we fail to obey God's command, "Be still and know that I am God"? Isn't it amazing that as soon as the couple became still, everything made sense?

But according to verse 35, that wasn't the only thing that helped them finally see the truth. At the end of their account, they told the disciples *what things were done in the way, and how he was known of them in breaking of bread.* Interesting, don't you think? Jesus sat down at the table, broke up a few pieces of bread, and all of a sudden, the Emmaus couple knew exactly who He was. Why was that? What was it about the breaking of bread that confirmed Jesus' identity in their hearts? Do you want to know what I think? (If not, you might just want to skip ahead a little because I'm going to tell you anyway.) I believe that this couple was present at the feeding of the five thousand. I think they had seen Him break bread before. I believe that the action was so familiar to them that as soon as He began tearing the bread into pieces, their minds wondered, "Where have I seen this before?" And by the time it clicked, Jesus was gone. Talk about déjà vu! Do I have any evidence for this? No, not really, but it makes sense, doesn't it?

One last thing I want to point out before moving on to the next set of characters. *And they rose up the same hour, and returned to Jerusalem.* They had just walked seven miles! I'm a regular hiker, and I can attest that's a long haul. I believe the longest hike I've personally ever been on was twelve miles. Again, I'm no math whiz, but I'm pretty sure seven miles there and seven miles back equals a fourteen-mile round trip. But as soon as they realized what was going on, they ran back to Jerusalem. They didn't crawl. They didn't walk. They ran. I guess it's just proof that renewed hope can put a spring in your step.

THE WOMEN

In the end of the sabbath, as it began to dawn toward the first day of the week, came Mary Magdalene and the other Mary to see the sepulchre. (Matthew 28:1)

148

And when the sabbath was past, Mary Magdalene, and Mary the mother of James, and Salome, had bought sweet spices, that they might come and anoint him. (Mark 16:1)

Now upon the first day of the week, very early in the morning, they came unto the sepulchre, bringing the spices which they had prepared, and certain others with them. . .It was Mary Magdalene and Joanna, and Mary the mother of James, and other women that were with them, which told these things unto the apostles. (Luke 24:1,10)

The first day of the week cometh Mary Magdalene early, when it was yet dark, unto the sepulchre, and seeth the stone taken away from the sepulchre. (John 20:1)

As you can see, there appears to be some contradiction in how many women were actually at the tomb of Jesus and who those women were. But I assure you, the Bible has no contradictions, but rather each human instrument was allowed to tell the story from his own perspective. God is the author of the Bible, but He entrusted men with the task of penning the words, and in such, He gave them the opportunity to allow their own personalities and points of view to shine through. And take it from a writer, the viewpoint is vital.

A few years ago, Jason and I were in an automobile accident. We were on our way to a church function and needed to make a quick stop on the way. As the traffic light before us turned green, we started across the busy intersection. A blur caught the corner of my eye, and in a split second, I realized that an SUV was barreling toward us, its driver obviously unaware of the red light in his direction. In my jumble of thoughts, one word surfaced: "NOOOOOOO!" Jason slammed on the brakes. The SUV caught the front corner of our truck and immediately flipped and flipped and flipped again.

When the vehicle finally stopped tumbling, it was sitting in the median and facing the opposite direction. We inched our truck over to the side of the road in hopes to avoid another accident from our presence in the middle of the intersection. After making sure I was okay, Jason went over to check on the driver of the other vehicle. I sat down on the grass (my legs would no longer hold me up) and stared at the scene before me. I stared at the battered SUV. I stared at the intersection. I stared at the flashing lights of the emergency vehicles. I honestly have no idea how long the entire ordeal lasted, but it seemed like a very long time.

After we had told our story to the policeman and watched our truck as it was loaded onto the tow truck, my parents arrived in response to our call. That evening as I was giving them the details of the accident, I described the flipping of the SUV and how it had finally ended up upside down in the median. Jason promptly corrected me, "It wasn't upside down. It was on its side."

"No, it wasn't," I replied. "It was upside down. I remember. I stared at it for what seemed like forever."

"No, Dana," he said patiently. "It was lying on the driver's side."

"No," I argued. "The EMS pulled the driver out the driver's side door. I remember. I watched them."

Again, Jason shook his head. "No, sweetie. They pulled him out through the windshield of the car. I know. I was standing right there."

He was standing right there. He was there the entire time. But still, I was positive about what I had seen. If I had taken a lie detector test right then, it would have registered that I was telling the truth. I believed what I was saying because I was reporting the events as I remembered them. Unfortunately, after hearing other reports, it turns out Jason was right. The car had landed on the driver's side, and the driver had been pulled from the car through the windshield. How could I have gotten my facts so mixed up? Evidently, in my state of anxiety, my perspective was a bit flawed.

I'm not suggesting that any of the passages in the Bible are flawed because the men who penned them had flawed perspectives. I'm merely trying to point out that perspective makes a big difference in a story. Each writer was writing from his experience, and when that happens, facts are bound to come across a little different. The important thing to remember is to keep the main thing the main thing. Whether there was one Mary at the tomb or a large group of women doesn't really matter. What matters is what we can learn from their discovery.

One thing we know for sure about these women is that they were going to the tomb expecting to find a dead body. Their mission was to anoint the body of Jesus with spices and oils. It was part of a burial ritual to show respect to the deceased and to curb the smell of the decaying flesh. This act alone tells us that they did not believe Christ's promise that He would rise again. They had no faith that He would do what He said He would

151

do. And that lack of faith planted a seed of worry—*And they said among themselves, Who shall roll us away the stone from the door of the sepulchre? (Mark 16:3)* On their way, they realized they had a serious problem. They knew soldiers had been placed at the tomb to protect against anyone getting in. . .or out. And even if the soldiers were willing to let the women in to perform such a task, would the men be able to move the stone? We have no idea how many men it took to roll the stone into place. How many would it take to roll it away? (And yes, that's a bit of a trick question, but we're not to that point in the story yet, so be patient. We'll get there.)

These well-meaning women faced the same problem that many of us face today. They allowed their feelings to overshadow their knowledge. They allowed their logic to undermine God's promise. And as a result, worry crept in. Oh, how many hours of our lives do we waste worrying about things that never happen? Unaware of its cost, we allow worry to dominate our minds and hearts, and all the while it saps us of strength, energy, joy, and peace. These women knew better. They had sat under Jesus' teaching. They had learned at His feet. They had witnessed His miracles. They had claimed His promises. But when things didn't feel right, when things didn't work out the way they had imagined, they lost sight of those promises. May I ask you a very serious question? If we can't trust God's promises, is there anything we can be sure of? God's promises are everything. Without them, how can we possibly hope to get through this life? When troubles arise, if we can't cling to His promises, what can we do? We find ourselves like these women, conferring amongst

HE'S STILL WORKING MIRACLES

themselves about how they were going to fulfill their plan. They had no idea that the stone had already been moved. They were blinded by their doubt. Much like Mary Magdalene was when Jesus appeared to her in the flesh.

The first day of the week cometh Mary Magdalene early, when it was yet dark, unto the sepulchre, and seeth the stone taken away from the sepulchre. Then she runneth, and cometh to Simon Peter, and to the other disciple, whom Jesus loved, and saith unto them, They have taken away the LORD out of the sepulchre, and we know not where they have laid him. Peter therefore went forth, and that other disciple, and came to the sepulchre. So they ran both together: and the other disciple did outrun Peter, and came first to the sepulchre. And he stooping down, and looking in, saw the linen clothes lying; yet went he not in. Then cometh Simon Peter following him, and went into the sepulchre, and seeth the linen clothes lie, And the napkin, that was about his head, not lying with the linen clothes, but wrapped together in a place by itself. Then went in also that other disciple, which came first to the sepulchre, and he saw, and believed. For as yet they knew not the scripture, that he must rise again from the dead. Then the disciples went away again unto their own home. But Mary stood without at the sepulchre weeping: and as she wept, she stooped down, and looked into the sepulchre, And seeth two angels in white sitting, the one at the head, and the other at the feet, where the body of Jesus had lain. And they say unto her, Woman, why weepest thou? She saith unto them, Because they have taken away my LORD, and I know not where they have laid

153

him. And when she had thus said, she turned herself back, and saw Jesus standing, and knew not that it was Jesus. Jesus saith unto her, Woman, why weepest thou? whom seekest thou? She, supposing him to be the gardener, saith unto him, Sir, if thou have borne him hence, tell me where thou hast laid him, and I will take him away. Jesus saith unto her, Mary. She turned herself, and saith unto him, Rabboni; which is to say, Master. Jesus saith unto her, Touch me not; for I am not yet ascended to my Father: but go to my brethren, and say unto them, I ascend unto my Father, and your Father; and to my God, and your God. Mary Magdalene came and told the disciples that she had seen the LORD, and that he had spoken these things unto her. (John 20:1-18)

Can you imagine? Jesus was standing there before her very eyes, and she didn't recognize him. Grief and doubt can blind us to the most obvious things. Things that we know without a shadow of a doubt become hazy when doubt steps in. You see, Mary believed in Christ. She did. But like so many others, she didn't truly believe in His power. Sure, He could work miracles for others, but not for Himself. Sure He could raise others from the dead, but not Himself. She put a limit on God just like we often do. We know who God is and what He is capable of, yet when circumstances seem hopeless, we throw up our hands and say, "Well, this one's too big for you, God. What am I going to do now?" My friend, hear me loud and clear—God has no limits! There is nothing that He cannot do, and until we believe in that power, we will never experience God like we want to. Sure, we can be saved, but we'll never see His full power in our own lives until we acknowledge who He is and what He is capable of.

I can imagine Mary thinking, "Who is this man? He looks like Jesus, but He couldn't be." But then something wonderful happened: Jesus spoke her name. He could have been aggravated by her lack of faith and gone elsewhere to show Himself to someone who would recognize Him. He could have berated her for her worry. He could have done a lot of things, but He chose to do the one thing He knew would identify Himself. In His sweet, tender voice, He called out, "Mary." She didn't have to hear it twice. Where His appearance had failed, His voice had succeeded. She knew that voice, especially when He spoke her name. Aren't you grateful for all the times God has called your name?

When you were confused or downhearted.

When you were alone or afraid.

When you felt that no one in the world cared about you.

Isn't it amazing how our names on the lips of the Savior can make everything right?

Despite her other mistakes, we have to give Mary credit for one thing. When Peter and John went home, Mary decided to stay. She stuck around to see what would happen next. Because of that, she was the first one to see the resurrected Christ. What an honor! It pays to wait on God. Even when things look impossible, God has a plan. The trouble is that we run away (like Peter and John) before God reveals the next step. It's like walking away from a good book and never reading the ending. Why do we do that? Don't we want to know what's going to happen next? Mary did.

Whatever you may be facing today, I urge you to wait it out. Whether it's a dead-end job, a loveless relationship, a dying ministry, or an important decision, follow Mary's example. Stick around. Wait. Talk to the Gardner. Listen to the voice of the Savior. But whatever you do, don't walk off. Your story's not over yet. There is much to be revealed!

THE DISCIPLES

When Jesus met with the women after His resurrection, He gave strict instructions for them to go tell the disciples what they had seen and heard. My favorite of these passages is in Mark 16:7: *But go your way, tell his disciples and Peter that he goeth before you into Galilee: there shall ye see him, as he said unto you.* Did you notice the wording Mark used? Tell the disciples **and Peter**. And Peter? Wasn't Peter one of the disciples? Yes, he was. Doesn't it seem odd that Jesus would single him out? Maybe a little, but I think Jesus had his reasons.

If you'll think back to before the crucifixion, Jesus told the disciples that all of them would abandon Him in the end. Peter didn't like this proclamation. In fact, he told Jesus in no uncertain terms that he would stand with Him no matter what. He claimed he would die for Christ. Unfortunately, we know the Bible spells out every painful detail of Peter's three-fold denial of Christ. We also know that Peter went out and wept bitterly. It's very possible that at the time of the resurrection, Peter no longer considered himself one of Jesus' disciples. In his mind, he hadn't earned such recognition. He didn't deserve such a place of honor.

When Jesus singled out Peter in His instructions to the women, I think He was trying to make a point. First off, I see it as a sign to Peter that all had been forgiven. I'm sure Peter did a lot of praying while he was weeping, and I imagine that the words "I'm sorry" escaped his lips countless times. By saying "and Peter," I believe Jesus was letting Peter know that everything was going to be alright. While his sin was not excused, it was forgiven.

Secondly, Jesus' words strike me as a proclamation of a promise kept. In essence, Jesus was saying, "Tell Peter that even though he didn't keep his promise to me, I'm still keeping my promise to him. I told him I would rise again, and that's exactly what I've done." What a blessing to know that God's promise-keeping isn't dependent on ours. What if God broke a promise to us every time we broke one to Him? How awful life would be! I'm ashamed to say that I haven't kept many of the promises I've made to the Lord. I didn't mean to break them, but temptation stepped in, the flesh grew weak, and before I knew what was happening, I, like Peter, was running off to weep over my failure. Considering the many times I've let God down, I wouldn't blame Him at all if He gave up on me. But He hasn't, and He won't. Despite my many failures, I can testify today that God has never, ever broken one of His promises to me. His Word is true, and He will be faithful, even when we aren't.

Thirdly, I see Peter singled out to remind us that nothing can separate us from the love of God. When we fail, not only does God still keep His promises, but His love for us never changes. No matter how far we've fallen or how often we've stumbled, God loves us with an undying love. We can't do anything to make Him love us more, but neither can we do anything to make Him love us less. When Peter denied Jesus, Jesus looked right at Peter. He knew what the disciple had done, and yes, He was disappointed. But he didn't love Peter any less. Our sin disappoints God. It even angers Him. But the Bible makes it clear that God's love for us is unchanging. *For I am persuaded, that neither death, nor life, nor angels, nor principalities, nor powers, nor things present, nor things to come, Nor height, nor depth, nor any other creature, shall be able to separate us from the love of God, which is in Christ Jesus our Lord.*[1]

Lastly, I believe Jesus wanted Peter to know that he still belonged. Even though Peter didn't feel worthy to be a disciple, Jesus assured Peter that he could still be used. I have often wondered why God would use me to write books and articles to bring glory to His name. So many times I feel like a hypocrite telling others how to live a worry-free life and how to leave their problems at the throne of God. Time and time again, I fail to practice what I "preach," and yet God still chooses to use me. When I ask Him why He would use me when there are so many others He could use, His answer amazes me. "Because, Dana, you need to be used." He's right! (Well, duh, of course He's right.) He doesn't need to use me, but I need to be used. When God writes through me, the impact of His teaching is overwhelming. I'm not just writing to help and encourage others. I'm getting help and encouragement at the same time. God blesses me so that I can pass on those blessings to others. What a joy and privilege! Jesus didn't have to use Peter. He had other disciples. But Peter needed to be used, so Jesus made certain he knew that he still belonged. He was still a usable vessel.

The women, after seeing and worshiping Jesus, rushed off and told the disciples just as Jesus had instructed them. Can you imagine the disciples reactions to such wonderful news? Were they elated? Did they throw a party? Did they go out and spread the news? In a word, no. Their response was unbelief. Luke put is this way: *And their words seemed to them as idle tales, and they believed them not.* The women came. They told what they had seen, what the angels had said, and what Jesus Himself had said. And the disciples said, "Whatever!" The book of Mark tells us that not only did the disciples not believe when the women came, but they didn't believe when the couple from the Emmaus Road came either. Two groups of people were telling them the same thing, yet the disciples shook their heads and muttered, "Nah, it couldn't be." Talk about blinded!

Afterward he appeared unto the eleven as they sat at meat, and upbraided them with their unbelief and hardness of heart, because they believed not them which had seen him after he was risen. (Mark 16:14)

Mary Magdalene may not have gotten a reprimand for her lack of faith, but these disciples sure did. Notice, though, that it doesn't say that Jesus was upset with them because they hadn't believed *Him.* The Bible says that He upbraided (which basically means rebuked or fussed at) the disciples because they didn't believe *them* which had seen Jesus after He had risen.

They didn't believe the women and the two from Emmaus Road. That's what Jesus was upset about. Believe it or not, Jesus is very protective of His children.

Still, with Jesus standing there in their midst, the disciples didn't recognize Him. They thought He was a ghost. How strange it is that they could believe in a ghost but not in a resurrected Savior.

And as they thus spake, Jesus himself stood in the midst of them, and saith unto them, Peace be unto you. But they were terrified and affrighted, and supposed that they had seen a spirit. And he said unto them, Why are ye troubled? and why do thoughts arise in your hearts? Behold my hands and my feet, that it is I myself: handle me, and see; for a spirit hath not flesh and bones, as ye see me have. And when he had thus spoken, he shewed them his hands and his feet. And while they yet believed not for joy, and wondered, he said unto them, Have ye here any meat? And they gave him a piece of a broiled fish, and of an honeycomb. And he took it, and did eat before them. And he said unto them, These are the words which I spake unto you, while I was yet with you, that all things must be fulfilled, which were written in the law of Moses, and in the prophets, and in the psalms, concerning me. Then opened he their understanding, that they might understand the scriptures, And said unto them, Thus it is written, and thus it behooved Christ to suffer, and to rise from the dead the third day: And that repentance and remission of sins should be preached in his name among all nations, beginning at Jerusalem. (Luke 24:36-45)

Jesus appeared before them, and they didn't get it. He spoke to them, and they didn't get it. He showed them His pierced hands and feet, but they merely gaped at Him with blank stares. He ate before them, giving them evidence that He was indeed alive and not a spirit, but they still didn't believe. Finally, He gave them a brief history lesson which could be summed up like this: "Okay, boys, do you remember what I told you was going to happen to me? Do you remember the Bible? Okay, good, let's go back to the beginning and see what it says. Didn't the Bible say that I would suffer and die? Didn't it describe my piercings and even my words? Didn't everything happen just the way it's described in Scripture? Do you understand what I'm telling you?" And finally, they did.

Has God ever beat you over the head with the Scriptures? You've studied the Word. You've memorized verses. You know God's promises. Yet in difficult times, you tend to get spiritual amnesia.

"Lord, this is a bad situation. Nothing good could ever come from this."

To which the Lord responds, "Remember Romans 8:28?"

"Oh yeah!"

"Lord, why are you doing this to me? Why are you allowing such heartache? Are you trying to hurt me?"

And the Lord's response?

"In Jeremiah, I made it very clear that I have plans for you, and those plans are not intended for evil, but for your good."

"Right."

Do you see how easy it is to become so wrapped up in the emotions of our circumstances that we fail to see the truth. . .even when it's staring us in the face.

Before moving on to the next section, I want to say a brief word about Thomas. In many ways, I feel sorry for Thomas. Somehow, throughout the years, he was dubbed with the title "Doubting Thomas." You see, he wasn't in the upper room when Jesus first appeared to the disciples. So when he met up with them, and they told him they'd seen Jesus, he didn't believe. It wasn't until Jesus appeared to Thomas and invited him to touch His wounds that Thomas actually believed. And so, forevermore, Thomas will be known as "Doubting Thomas," but is that really fair? We just saw that the other disciples didn't believe until they saw Jesus for themselves. Didn't they doubt just as much as Thomas did? It sure looks like it to me. But Thomas, bless his heart, was singled out in this instance and because of his unbelief, he received a nickname that has outlived him. Judas will always be the betrayer. Peter will always be the denier. And Thomas will always be the doubter. I don't know about you, but I'm not fond of any of those nicknames. Nevertheless, we are often known by our actions. What will people call you?

JESUS, THE RISEN LAMB

Naturally, we can't tell the story of the resurrection without talking about the main character: Jesus. Ironically, there is little detail in the Bible about what actually took place during Jesus' three days in the grave. We've already seen several accounts of things He

162

did after He arose, but what happened while He was dead and why was it three days before He arose?

Let's deal with the second question first. To begin with, prophecy stated that Jesus would die, be buried, then rise again after three days. The resurrection took place just as prophecy said it would, thus proving the inerrancy of God's Word. The significance of the three days, I believe, is two-fold. If Jesus had risen sooner, it could be argued that He wasn't actually dead but merely unconscious and eventually revived by the coolness of the tomb. It is logical to conclude that a man could survive without food or water for a couple of days. So, if He had risen sooner, skeptics would deny His actual death. On the other hand, if Jesus had stayed in the grave any longer, His body would have begun to decay, much like Lazarus' body, which had been in the grave for four days.

As for what took place during the time Jesus was dead, that's a bit tricky. There are various theories and suppositions, but the Biblical evidence for many such theories is sketchy. The fact of the matter is that the Bible gives a few details here and there, and it is up to us to piece together the facts as best as we can without doing damage to the Word of God. That being the case, I will attempt to give you a brief chronology of the events along with Bible passages to support my claims.

At some point during those three days, Jesus descended into the depths of the earth to a place known as Hades or Sheol. At that time, Hades was divided into two parts: Paradise and Hell. For those who died believing in Jesus (like the thief on the cross), their bodies were buried, and their spirits descended into

Paradise, which was a temporary holding place for those who believed. Those who died without faith in Christ were delivered into Hell (which is where we see the rich man in Luke 16) and were cut off from those in Paradise.

During this visit, I believe—based on Biblical passages—that He accomplished two things. First off, He preached to a group of unbelievers. I Peter 3:18-20 tells us, *For Christ also hath once suffered for sins, the just for the unjust, that he might bring us to God, being put to death in the flesh, but quickened by the Spirit: By which also he went and preached unto the spirits in prison; Which sometime were disobedient, when once the longsuffering of God waited in the days of Noah, while the ark was a preparing, wherein few, that is, eight souls were saved by water.* Now, the exact identity of those to whom He preached is not mentioned, nor do we know what He said to them. After all, it's not like He was preaching to them so that they would get saved. They were in Hell. Salvation was no longer available to them. Perhaps, He was simply giving them the message that everything He had said was true and had come to pass. Whatever the case, it is clear that He had something important to say.

Also, during this time, He freed those who were in Paradise. With His death accomplished and His resurrection imminent, there was no longer a need for a holding place. These souls could not previously enter into Heaven because the blood of the spotless Lamb of God had not yet been presented as payment for their sins, but all that was about to change. Ephesians 4:8-10 gives us this account. *Wherefore he saith, When he ascended up on high, he led captivity captive, and gave gifts unto men. (Now that he ascended, what is it but that he also descended first into the lower parts of the earth? He that descended is the same also that ascended up far above all heavens, that he might fill all things.)*

This is where things get a bit strange. Jesus told the thief on the cross, "To day shalt thou be with me in paradise," which leads me to believe that Jesus descended into the depths of the earth on the very same day on which He died. However, the spirits that Jesus set free couldn't ascend to Heaven until Jesus delivered His blood to the mercy seat, which by all accounts He didn't do until after His resurrection. So, what happened to these spirits during that time? Where did they go? What did they do? It is possible some of them returned to their bodies which had been resurrected from the grave.

And the graves were opened; and many bodies of the saints which slept arose, And came out of the graves after his resurrection, and went into the holy city, and appeared unto many. (Matthew 27:52-53)

Can you imagine? Not only was Jesus once again alive and walking around, but many of the saints were as well. Talk about night of the living dead! Creepy. Again, exactly who these saints were and what happened to them after they went to the holy city we're left to guess. To my knowledge, the Bible never speaks of them again. But, based on what the Bible does say, we can know that, at some point, those in Paradise were transported to Heaven. Whether some of them ascended bodily, I have no idea.

There is also conjecture that during His trip to the underworld, Jesus battled Satan for the keys to Death and Hell. There is no Biblical proof for this, and if you think about it, the theory is flawed. Satan never had the keys of Death and Hell. Jesus has always been in control and therefore has always had the keys. In Revelation 1, Jesus states, *I am he that liveth, and was dead; and, behold, I am alive for evermore, Amen; and have the keys of hell and of death.* Notice, He said, "I have the keys" not "I've won the keys." If anything, after Jesus finished preaching to those lost souls and just before He led captivity captive, He looked Satan right in the eye, jingled the keys in His hand, and said, "Oh, and by the way, these are mine!" Jesus was victorious over Death and Hell! That battle was fought and won on the cross. Hallelujah for that! For it is that victory that opened up eternal life to us. Because of Jesus' death and resurrection, we all have the choice to live with Him forever in Heaven. We need only believe in Him.

And because of that, I like to think of this particular story as the miracle that produces miracles, because salvation is just that—a miracle!

Section Five:

Miracles

of

Love

HE'S STILL WORKING MIRACLES

Chapter Nine:

FOOTPRINTS ON THE WATER

And straightway Jesus constrained his disciples to get into a ship, and to go before him unto the other side, while he sent the multitudes away. And when he had sent the multitudes away, he went up into a mountain apart to pray: and when the evening was come, he was there alone. But the ship was now in the midst of the sea, tossed with waves: for the wind was contrary. And in the fourth watch of the night Jesus went unto them, walking on the sea. And when the disciples saw him walking on the sea, they were troubled, saying, It is a spirit; and they cried out for fear. But straightway Jesus spake unto them, saying, Be of good cheer; it is I; be not afraid. And Peter answered him and said, Lord, if it be thou, bid me come unto thee on the water. And he said, Come. And when Peter was come down out of the ship, he walked on the water, to go to Jesus. But when he saw the wind boisterous, he was afraid; and beginning to sink, he cried, saying, Lord, save me. And immediately Jesus stretched forth his hand, and caught him, and said unto him, O thou of little faith, wherefore didst thou doubt? And when they were come into the ship, the wind ceased. Then they that were in the ship came and worshipped him, saying, Of a truth thou art the Son of God. - Matthew 14:22-33

Several years ago, Jason and I had the opportunity to go on a Disney cruise to the Bahamas. I had never been on a cruise before and had only been on a boat a few times in my life. Needless to say, I was a little nervous, but overall, my excitement outweighed my anxiety. For the first few days of the voyage, I was delighted to discover that I could barely detect the motion of the ship. I didn't feel queasy or motion sick in any way. In fact, if not for the times when I looked out and saw the passing ocean, I would not have even thought we were moving. That is, until the last day of the cruise.

As long as I live, I don't think I will ever forget that day. I woke to an aching head and a sloshing stomach. The calm seas had departed, and in their place were waters churned by an oncoming storm. The sky was cloudy and dark even though it was well past daybreak. The wind whipped, and the rain fell. But above all, the boat rocked.

I tried everything I could think of to keep my stomach from recoiling. I took medicine, but that did not sit well. I tried to eat, but that sat even worse, especially since the entire time I was eating, I had a stellar view of the water rising and falling through the large round window in the dining room. Yes, the boat was tipping so severely that the water was going more than halfway up the window as we shifted one way and then totally disappearing from view as we shifted the other. If that weren't enough to make me sick, what happened next certainly was.

To distract ourselves from the nausea and to entertain ourselves during the storm, Jason and I decided to watch an animated movie showing in the theater. It seemed like a good idea until the moment I realized that the movie screen was a hanging screen which means it was not secured to the floor in any way. As the boat rocked back and forth, the movie screen shifted from side to side. I didn't know which was worst: the swaying of the movie screen, the rocking of the boat, or the churning of my stomach, but I soon found out.

As I jumped to my feet with my hand over my mouth, I sought the nearest exit. I was mortified to discover that every available surface of the movie theater was covered with people. Every seat was filled, and groups of people cluttered the steps and walkways. As best I could, I maneuvered around the many obstacles and made my way out of the theater, praying that I would find a restroom in time. Let's just say, I did... sort of.

Because of the rough seas that day, it took several days before I could walk on dry land without swaying and practically falling over. Of all the happy memories I have from that trip, it is the last day that stands out the most. I can now say that I know all too well the reality of being in the midst of the sea and tossed with waves. Not only in the physical sense, mind you, but in the spiritual sense as well. I've struggled in the sea of decision, tossed about by confusion. I've floundered around in the sea of sickness, overcome by the waves of frustration. All in all, more times than I can count, I've found myself in the midst of the sea of circumstances, tossed about by hopelessness. Surrounded by a strong wind and a battered vessel, there have been times I've lost sight of everything but the storm. In times such as this, I have no answers, only questions.

WHY AM I GOING THROUGH THIS STORM?

I'm sure the disciples were confounded by the storm. After all, they were following Jesus' command. He had instructed them to go to the other side of the sea, and they hastened to obey. No arguments. No complaints. He said "go," and they went. Unfortunately, obedience to God's commands does not guarantee us an absence of storms. Take it from someone who knows.

A few years ago, I was living the life of which I'd always dreamed (minus the endless wealth, of course). I was happily married to my best friend. I had a home of my own, a loving family, possessions above and beyond what I needed, a good church, and a job I loved. Sure, as a Christian school teacher, I didn't make much money, but I didn't mind. I enjoyed my career and looked forward to each day. You can imagine my surprise and dismay when God began burdening my heart about leaving my teaching job to pursue a career in writing. Sadly, it took some hardy persuasion (and serious unsettling) before I surrendered to God's will and walked away from the only job I had ever wanted to do.

In my first few months as a writer, I had great dreams of writing books that would find themselves on every bestsellers list. After taking some classes, I felt ready to tackle this new career, but it didn't take long for the reality to set in—writing is hard work! Day after day, I poured my heart and soul into my new craft only to be met with rejection after rejection. After three months, I still hadn't made a dime. Little did I know that things were about to get very interesting.

My husband, Jason, arrived home from work one afternoon with the bombshell that he no longer had a job. He worked for a local soft drink company, delivering beverages to businesses. It wasn't a great job, but for the most part, he enjoyed it and brought home a pretty good income. The company, however, had very strict rules about traffic violations. Without going into detail, I'll just say that Jason unwittingly broke one of those rules, and with that, he was let go. He was discouraged, and I was devastated. What were we going to do?

Thankfully, the Lord opened the door for Jason to go back to work at a company he had worked with previously. This meant, however, a serious drop in pay from where he had been. Within just a few months, our income had been cut in half. For the life of me, I couldn't figure out what God was doing. Was he punishing us, and if so, why? I had followed His directions. I was doing His will. We were faithful in attending church and lived wholesome lives. Why were we facing such a storm? Unfortunately, no answers were forthcoming. Only more questions.

HOW AM I GOING TO MAKE IT THROUGH?

The disciples had rowed for nine hours and had covered less than three miles. Three miles in nine hours! Don't you know they were exhausted? I can't imagine the strength it must have taken to keep that ship on course in the midst of such an awesome storm. And to maintain that strength for nine hours is simply amazing and a testament to the abilities these men had as fishermen. Still, for all their strength, they couldn't make it across. I can kind of relate.

A couple of years back, our church youth group went on a whitewater rafting trip down the Nantahala River. Assistant youth leaders at the time, Jason and I were privileged to accompany the group. Well, Jason felt privileged; I felt obligated. . .and terrified. I had never done anything like rafting, and water and I are not the best of friends. But since this trip was for our youth, I decided to face my fears. If only I had known what I was in for, I probably would have stayed home.

The first thing I found out, to my horror, was that we were not supposed to sit in the boat but rather on the side of the boat. Say what? This, to me, seemed like a very precarious position to be in and made me all the more likely to fall off the boat. There is an inflatable bar that runs across the boat under which you are supposed to put your feet for support. I had my feet wedged in there so far that they went numb within a few minutes. Whether that was from lack of circulation or the freezing water I can't say, but at the time, I didn't care. Right then, my only priority was to stay in the boat.

The next thing I learned was how to row. When I say I learned, what I mean is that my brain received the instructions. I must admit, however, that there seemed to be some difficulty with the transfer of that information from my brain to my body. I held my paddle correctly, with one hand firmly grasping the T-handle and the other closer to the end of the paddle. I excelled at paddling forward through smooth waters. Where I ran into trouble was when we hit rapids, and it was necessary for us to fight both with and against the current. The biggest challenge for me, it seemed, was the back paddle. I can't tell you how many times our guide would yell for everyone to back paddle, and it would take striking the paddle of the person in front of me several times before I realized I was paddling the wrong way. I know he had to grow tired of me saying, "Sorry, sorry."

There were four people in our boat, but I confess, by the end of the eight-mile run, I was sure I had been paddling alone. I was exhausted. My feet and legs were numb. My arms were shaking from the exertion, and my hands were cramped from holding the paddle. The fatigue I felt astounded me, and I wanted nothing more than to crawl into my nice soft bed and sleep for a week.

But as long as those few hours seemed and as tired as I felt, I'm sure it was nothing compared to what the disciples were facing that evening on the Galilean seas. To their advantage, they, at least, knew how to row, but in waters so contrary, I doubt it mattered. For every stroke forward, the seas pushed them three strokes back. The winds carried them one way as the churning waters carried them another. If they had had time to think, I'm sure several questions would have come to mind, the most prevalent being, "How are we going to get through this?"

In the years since our diminishing income, there have been many times I've lifted my voice to Heaven crying, "God, how are we going to make it through?" From where I'm standing, the situation looks hopeless. Like the disciples, I've used my talents and abilities to "get to the other side," but despite my hard work, it seems I never gain any ground. Even now, money is tight, my strength is nearly gone, and the waves seem to grow larger every day. That realization leads me to my next question.

WHERE ARE YOU, GOD?

Jesus had sent the disciples on ahead, but there's no indication that He told them where He was going. As far as we know, they had no idea where He was. They only knew where He wasn't (or at least, that's what they thought). You see, in our darkest storms, it's so easy to lose sight of God's promises, especially the one that says, *I will never leave thee, nor forsake thee.*[1]

Where is God? He's right here with us. He is watching, and in the case of the disciples, I believe He was also praying a prayer that He Himself would answer. He knew what they were facing. He was on that mountaintop praying and interceding for them as it says in Hebrews 7:24-25: *But this man, because he continueth ever, hath an unchangeable priesthood. Wherefore he is able also to save them to the uttermost that come unto God by him, seeing he ever liveth to make intercession for them.*

No matter how alone we may feel, it is imperative that we remember that God is still with us. He has never left our side, and He never will.

IF GOD IS WATCHING, WHY DOES HE WAIT?

It's a fair question, and as we already mentioned, God is not offended by our questions. He only takes offense when we demand answers or when we demand that He answer according to our timetable. He is a gracious and merciful God and does not long to see us suffer. So if that's the case, why doesn't He answer our prayers and meet our needs right away? Why does He wait until the money is gone, the loved one has died, or all hope seems lost?

Though you hear nothing, he is speaking. Though you see nothing, he is acting. With God there are no accidents. Every incident is intended to bring us closer to him.[2]

There is a reason. God has a plan, and while we find it inconvenient and even painful to wait, we can rest assured that God has our best interests at heart. His actions (or inaction) are purposed to teach us to depend on Him and delight in Him.

As a child, I had a natural inclination for playing the piano. I had just enough of an ear for music to pick out simple melodies and string them together into a pleasing tune. When my parents signed me up for piano lessons, I was thrilled. In my childlike mind, I would be playing like Beethoven in no time. Such, however, was not the case. In fact, the first few years of lessons consisted of boring scales, piddly songs, and a number of different fingering exercises. I was growing increasingly frustrated until one day my teacher announced that I was going to learn my first "real" song. My instructor opened my book to the song she had prepared for me and began to play. It was really simple and sounded almost clunky to my ears. Still, it was a real song, and I was determined I was going to play it just like my teacher did. After all, it looked easy enough.

Well, it wasn't. It took me weeks of frustration and plunking down one note after another to get that song down to where it was at least recognizable. Nevertheless, the first time I played the song without making a mistake, my smile could not be contained. I had played a song, a real song. I had made music. Unfortunately, I was only able to take lessons for about six years, but in those years I learned a lot. I can now pick up a lesson book for beginners and play without pause. The notes and fingering come naturally to me. However, when faced with a more difficult piece, I have to make a decision to cast it aside or to spend the hours necessary to turn the mere notes into something much more pleasing to the ear. To make that decision, I have to believe that today's struggles will bring tomorrow's music.

Could that be why God is waiting? Is it possible He is allowing us to go through our current circumstances so that we can experience the sweet music that awaits on the other side? Whatever the reason, we can rest assured that He will make His presence known to us at the right time, just as He did with the disciples. *Be of good cheer; it is I; be not afraid.*

WALKING ON THE WATER

As I mentioned before, I haven't spent much time on a boat, but common sense tells me that during a storm, I'd be better off in the boat than in the sea. Right? As Max Lucado puts it, *Stepping onto a stormy sea is not a move of logic; it is a move of desperation.*[3]

That didn't stop Peter from making his bold request. The way Peter figured it, he was safer on the seas with Jesus than in the boat without Him. *And Peter*

178

answered him and said, Lord, if it be thou, bid me come unto thee on the water. I really don't know why it is that the disciples didn't recognize Jesus. My best guess would be that it was dark, and between the downpour of the rain and the flashes of lightning, visibility was poor. Additionally, His voice could have been drowned out (no pun intended) by the crashing of the waves and the thunder. I don't know, but I do know that Peter was skeptical, so he threw out a challenge. "Okay, if you're really who you say you are, let me walk on the water too." Brave or insane? Who's to say, but Peter didn't have time to think about it. No sooner had he issued the challenge than Jesus responded, "Come on." Jesus didn't have to honor this absurd request, but He did as an act of compassion.

I have to wonder, if the sea had been calm and no storm had been present, would Peter still have asked to walk on the water? I doubt it. That's the funny thing about storms. They urge us to take steps we never intended to take. In all his years as a fisherman, Peter had never walked on the sea before. I'm pretty sure he had never tried. Why? Because there was never a need. Often, storms coax us out of our comfort zones and prompt us to take a risk or to do the unexpected. Leaps of faith. Walks on the water. Call it what you will, but God does some of His best work through some of our fiercest storms.

Storms help us to see the precariousness of our situation. They open our eyes to the dangers around us. They remind us that our works and efforts offer as much resistance to the storm as an old, rugged fishing boat. They redirect our vision back to the only One who can save us from ourselves. And in that desperation, they give us the strength we need to step out in faith.

If Peter were here today and could give us one tip about walking on the water, I'm sure it would be this: focus! When race car drivers are interviewed, one question they are often asked is, "How do you stay off the wall?" Each time, the answer is the same: "Easy, I don't look at the wall." By looking at the things we don't want, we find ourselves pulled toward them. Our focus will determine our direction. Peter can testify. He started out strong. Placing his feet firmly on the churning waters. With a deep breath, he released his grip on the boat and took his first step, then another and another. Just as his fear began to subside, thunder boomed across the water, and lightning temporarily blinded him. When his vision returned, all he could see was the storm, and in that instant, his watery walkway became sinking sand.

Satan is a pro at distracting us from our true goals. The harder we try to focus on Christ and on living for Him, the more distractions the devil will throw our way. Over time, it becomes so difficult to focus, and just when we find ourselves getting back on track, Satan sends another snare across our paths. Just like Peter, we lose sight of our Source of strength and begin to sink under the weight of our circumstances. At that point, we often respond as Peter did, *Lord, save me!* After all, what else can we do? Peter was helpless. He knew he wouldn't survive without the Lord's aid. It's time we realized that we cannot save ourselves. Our strength is insufficient. We need a Savior.

Note that Jesus didn't hesitate to answer Peter's plea. He may have waited to show up on the water, but as soon as Peter cried, Jesus reached out to him. He pulled him up out of the sea and with a disappointed shake of His head proclaimed, *O ye of little faith*. I imagine those words stung Peter more than the pelting rain, but he couldn't deny the truth of them.

What about you?

Have you ever lost your faith? Focused on the wrong things? Struggled to find a way out of your current circumstances?

Blinded by the storm, it's easy to forget God's glowing resume, isn't it? Our God, the God of today, is the One who created all things. He is the One who parted the Red Sea. It was He who used a little shepherd boy to slay a mighty giant. He brought down the walls of Jericho, healed the sick, and raised Lazarus from the grave. Over and over again, He has proven His power and might, yet we can't help wondering if He can help us through our storms. Little faith, indeed. I fear far too many of us are reaching out to Jesus with one hand while clutching the boat with a white-knuckled grip of the other hand.

HELLO! WHAT JUST HAPPENED?

What we often forget about this story is that it takes place on the heels of the feeding of the five thousand. The disciples had just witnessed Jesus do something they had never dreamed possible. In fact, their twelve baskets of leftovers were still in the boat with them. Would God have provided their meal for tomorrow if He knew there wouldn't be one? Would He have sent the food knowing they'd never have a chance to eat it? Christian writer, Lynn Mosher, paints a beautiful picture of this account of spiritual amnesia.

The disciples fail to understand the meaning of the miracle of the loaves. Lacking insight into its significance hardens their hearts that Jesus has the power to do whatever they need. With the smell of fish still clinging to their fingertips and the bread crumbs still resting in the folds of their garments, they do not remember how those things got there. The bread merely filled their stomachs. Even though they take the baskets of leftover bread with them into the boat, they do not take the Bread of Life with them into their hearts. [4]

What about us? What's our excuse? We're surrounded by blessings, yet we accuse God of not providing. We have the receipts for bills paid despite the empty bank account. We have the Word of God with its recorded events of how God has seen His children through time and time again. We have God's promise that He is faithful. What more do we need? Why do we allow the storms of life to make us forget the truths that we know? Why do we allow them to shatter our faith?

Whenever I think of this story, I remember a picture I saw a few years ago. It displayed Jesus standing tall on the water, and Peter standing before Him with a children's swimming float around his middle and a cheesy grin on his face. At the time, it made me laugh, but the more I think about it, the more it makes me cringe because I see myself in that illustration. Faith doesn't involve safety nets, nor does it implement a backup plan. True faith requires us to lean wholly on Jesus and to release our grip on the boat.

You aren't truly trusting until you're slightly out of control—like Peter when he stepped out on the water. You aren't truly trusting until you've leaned so hard on Him that if you fell, you couldn't catch yourself. Trust means setting aside all secondary options, backup systems, and emergency parachutes. Trust says, "I've gone so far now that there's no return for me. If God doesn't save me and hold me up, I'll go under.[5]

Are you facing a storm today? If so, don't be afraid. Are you tired and weary from getting nowhere even though you've toiled and tried? Look to the Master. He's reaching out His hand. He bids you come. Take that first step out of the boat, and whatever you do, keep your eyes on Him. He'll keep you from going under.

HE'S STILL WORKING MIRACLES

Chapter Ten:

GOD FILLS EMPTY NETS

And it came to pass, that, as the people pressed upon him to hear the word of God, he stood by the lake of Gennesaret, And saw two ships standing by the lake: but the fishermen were gone out of them, and were washing their nets. And he entered into one of the ships, which was Simon's, and prayed him that he would thrust out a little from the land. And he sat down, and taught the people out of the ship. Now when he had left speaking, he said unto Simon, Launch out into the deep, and let down your nets for a draught. And Simon answering said unto him, Master, we have toiled all the night, and have taken nothing: nevertheless at thy word I will let down the net. And when they had this done, they inclosed a great multitude of fishes: and their net brake. And they beckoned unto their partners, which were in the other ship, that they should come and help them. And they came, and filled both the ships, so that they began to sink. When Simon Peter saw it, he fell down at Jesus' knees, saying, Depart from me; for I am a sinful man, O Lord. For he was astonished, and all that were with him, at the draught of the fishes which they had taken: And so was also James, and John, the sons of Zebedee, which were partners with Simon. And Jesus said unto Simon, Fear not; from henceforth thou shalt catch men. And when they had brought their ships to land, they forsook all, and followed him. - Luke 5:1-11

Have you ever felt like your work was in vain and that no matter how hard you tried, things just never worked out the way you intended? *Why bother?* you wonder. *After all my effort and hard work, I still have nothing to show for my efforts.* Believe me when I tell you that the disciples can relate. The Bible doesn't specify how many of the disciples were present during this event, but we do know that seven of the twelve disciples were fishermen, so it's likely there were at least that many. Unfortunately, in this situation, it didn't seem to matter how many of them there were. The results were the same. These skilled fishermen had fished all night and caught nothing.

Remember that these were not men out for a casual day of sport. They weren't fishing for the fun of it or for relaxation. They were working. Fishing was their trade. It was their income. It was their means of survival. No fish meant no money. No money meant big trouble for the disciples and their families. Hence their discouragement and frustration. Picture the disciples as they sat huddled cleaning their nets of the dirt and debris. Hunched shoulders. Pinched faces. Weary eyes. The disappointment practically oozed from them. I have no doubt they were exhausted, for even though they hadn't caught anything, they had still toiled the entire night. In other words, they had worked their full shift. They just didn't get paid for it.

My husband often teases me by saying, "For someone who works so hard, you sure don't make much money." I'm not offended by his statement because it's the truth. I spend my days pouring my heart and soul into books, articles, and devotions that only a few read and even fewer pay for. I work part-time as a college teacher. The pay is decent, but I work so few hours that it doesn't add up to much in the end. On the weekends, I serve as the teacher of our ladies' Sunday School class and the church pianist, for which I receive a small love offering. In my "free time," I clean house, cook meals, run errands, and perform any number of other tasks that may come up. Let me tell you, there are days when I fall into bed knowing that I've worked hard all day long but have nothing to show for my efforts. No income. No fruit. Nothing tangible that I cling to and find purpose in. Just frustration and disappointment. Questions that seem to have no answers and dreams that never seem to be fulfilled. But then Jesus speaks.

LAUNCH OUT A LITTLE

When Jesus stepped into Peter's boat and asked him to launch out a little, Peter didn't hesitate. I love the insight we have here into the compassion of Christ. The Bible says that the people were pressed upon Him. I imagine they were so close to Him that He could barely move. The problem was that only so many people could get that close, and with the multitude around Him, there were many others who couldn't even see or hear Him any longer. In His compassion and great wisdom, Jesus recognized the problem. He saw the needs of each individual, and He made a way for each one to be able to see and hear. By putting some distance between Himself and the crowd, He provided a solution to the impending problem. I firmly believe He had Peter launch out just enough to where the people could still see and hear Him but far enough out to where all the people could catch a glimpse of Him.

From there, Jesus taught the people. I wish the Bible had a record of what was taught that day, but I have a feeling it was the same thing that He taught in other passages of the Bible. Perhaps He spoke of His upcoming sacrifice on the cross. Maybe He talked of loving and forgiving one another. It's possible He gave details about His heavenly home. We really don't know what He said or how long He taught the people. What we do know, however, is that He was just beginning the lesson to the disciples.

LAUNCH OUT INTO THE DEEP

Now when he had left speaking, he said unto Simon, Launch out into the deep, and let down your nets for a draught. (Luke 5:4)

As difficult as it is for us to bear, sometimes God requires us to go a little farther before we reap His benefits. That may involve taking a risk, waiting for His timing, or even accepting that the thing we so greatly desire is not God's will for our lives. In any case, we'll never receive what God intends for us if we run from our problems. I'm certain that the last thing the disciples wanted to do was to go back out into the deepest part of the ocean and fish again. They were exhausted. They were frustrated. They wanted to walk away and leave their failure behind. They had no desire to sail right back to the source of their circumstances. But that's where God led them, and that's often where He'll lead us.

While it's imperative for our spiritual health that we do not dwell on our mistakes, it's equally important that we learn from them. God can use our failures and frustrations to teach us valuable lessons that we will never forget. In this scenario, the message Jesus was trying to get across was loud and clear—"without me ye can do nothing." Fishermen can't catch fish. Doctors can't perform surgery. Writers can't find the words. Bankers can't count. Were it not for the grace of God, we would all be in sad shape. It is God who gives us talents and abilities, and it is God who can withhold those things when He sees that we need an eye-opener.

In a sense, Peter understood that. His response, though weary, implies that he was resolved to obey Christ, even when He didn't agree or understand. That's a hard concept for many of us to grasp. Well, actually, it's more like Princess Mia states in the second Princess Diaries movie: "The concept is grasped; the execution is a little elusive."

As Christians, we know we should obey God no matter what, but when God's ways don't make sense, we find ourselves finding (or creating) loopholes for our disobedience. "Well, God can't really mean for me to leave my job. That's just not logical." "I'm sure it's not God's will for me to give all of that extra money to missions. It's probably just my own longing to help, but I have to be a good steward of God's money." In our confusion about God's purpose, we make excuses and run ourselves in circles trying to justify our choices to not follow His leading. My friends, may I ask you a very blunt question? Where does that disobedience usually lead? Faith doesn't require us to understand, only to obey, even if that obedience is plagued with weariness.

And Simon answering said unto him, Master, we have toiled all the night, and have taken nothing: nevertheless at thy word I will let down the net. (Luke 5:5)

Can I spell that out for you? "Been there. Done that. Caught nothing. But because You said so, we'll try it again." When was the last time we responded to God in that way, following His commands despite our weariness and previous failures? Chances are it hasn't been as recently as we would like. Is it any wonder then that we're frustrated over empty nets? If the disciples were going to catch fish, they had to get back to where the fish were. If we're going to receive God's blessings in our lives, in which direction should we head?

THE SPIRIT OF BROKENNESS

And when they had this done, they inclosed a great multitude of fishes: and their net brake. And they beckoned unto their partners, which were in the other ship, that they should come and help them. And they came, and filled both the ships, so that they began to sink. (Luke 5:6-7)

I'm sorry, but every time I read these verses, I can't help thinking of the old adage, "Be careful what you wish for." The disciples wanted fish. They got fish. . . a lot of fish. Two ships full of fish! Luke 6:38 tells us, *Give, and it shall be given unto you; good measure, pressed down, and shaken together, and running over, shall men give into your bosom. For with*

190

the same measure that ye mete withal it shall be measured to you again. Peter gave Jesus the use of his boat for the afternoon. He also gave his obedience in launching out to the deep. That giving was rewarded in a way that Peter had never imagined.

Good measure.

Pressed down.

Shaken together.

Running over.

What a blessing to see God's Word confirm God's Word! In one passage He tells what He will do, and in another passage we see the promise fulfilled. Ephesians 3:20 states the promise like this: *Now unto him that is able to do exceeding abundantly above all that we ask or think, according to the power that worketh in us.* Exceeding abundantly above what we could dream. That's what God wants for us. Unfortunately, it is often necessary for Him to first break us just as the nets were broken.

Peter's cry is a good indication of a spirit of brokenness. *When Simon Peter saw it, he fell down at Jesus' knees, saying, Depart from me; for I am a sinful man, O Lord. For he was astonished, and all that were with him, at the draught of the fishes which they had taken. (Luke 5:8-9)* A spirit of brokenness reveals both our unworthiness and the magnificence of God. It provides a state of teachability and pliability where God can mold our hearts into what He desires them to be. The spirit of brokenness occurs when we finally realize and admit that we cannot help ourselves and turn to God as our only source of comfort and provision. It involves the process of dying to our own ambitions and selfish pride and taking up the cross of Christ to bear with joy. In short, it's replacing our will with God's will. Only when we reach this point can God work fully in our lives.

As Christians, we pray over and over again for the Spirit to fill our lives and live through us. Please understand, this is different than the indwelling of the Spirit. When we accept Christ as our Savior, the Holy Spirit comes into our lives and dwells within us. That is the indwelling of the Spirit. Being filled with the Spirit takes place when we allow the Spirit to do more than just dwell. It occurs when we turn over control to Him and give Him access to every part of our being—our thoughts, our actions, our attitudes.

The problem often lies in the fact that we want to be filled, but we refuse to empty ourselves of all the filth that's accumulated within us. Elements like pride, bitterness, and resentment have deep roots in our hearts and minds and will not be easily persuaded to leave. But unless we empty ourselves of the bad, how can we expect to be filled with the good? It would be like having a cup full of mud and trying to fill that cup with crisp, clean water. It just doesn't work. That's where the spirit of brokenness comes into play, for it is at that point that we are finally willing to empty ourselves. And when we do, the Spirit is able to fill our hearts, and that's when we'll see God work His plan for our lives.

FISHERS OF MEN

And Jesus said unto Simon, Fear not; from henceforth thou shalt catch men. And when they had brought their ships to land, they forsook all, and followed him. (Luke 5:10b-11)

Because of what he had just seen, Peter considered himself unworthy to even be in Jesus' presence. I guess it's a good thing Jesus doesn't see us the same way we see ourselves. My interpretation of Jesus' statement to Peter would be this: "Yes, Peter, you are a sinful man, but I can use you anyway. You've seen what I can do with fish; now let me show you what I can do with men. Are you with me?"

The phrase "fishers of men" always reminds me of a chapel service I attended many years ago. At the time I was teaching a kindergarten class which attended chapel with the K-4. The three teachers took turns presenting the lesson for the weekly chapel services, and on this particular week, one of the K-4 teachers (who happened to be unmarried at the time) was teaching about this very miracle. When she reached this part of the story, she placed her hands on her hips, cocked her head and questioned the students, "So tell me, how do you catch a man?" The other teacher and I had a difficult time keeping straight faces. We knew what she meant, but the question, coming from an unmarried woman, came across in a totally different way. After chapel, we explained our grins. Needless to say, the poor woman was embarrassed but was able to laugh about the unintended meaning. Fishers of men, indeed.

In all seriousness, there is no greater calling than that. To be a fisher of men is to be a beacon in a dark world. To fish for men is to reach out to the lost. Beyond that, to be a fisher of men is a commandment given to each one of us. It is not a position reserved for the disciples. It is not the job of the preacher, missionary, or evangelist alone. We are all responsible for being witnesses for Christ. We are all required to share the good news. We have all been given the privilege of introducing others to our Lord and Savior. It is a task that should not be taken lightly, but it is one that should be performed with joy and excitement. We have a purpose. We have a calling. We weren't able to witness the miracle of the draught of fishes, but we have the opportunity to be first-hand witnesses of the miracles that God can work in the hearts of men.

You may be saying, "But I don't know if I can. I'm shy, and I don't really know the Bible that well." I understand. If that is your situation, I would advise you to get to know your Bible. God's Word is profitable for many things, and it will benefit you in all areas of your life. In the meantime, you can be a testimony for Christ by simply telling others what Christ has done for you. Don't you imagine the disciples told this story over and over again? When they didn't have the words to say, they could always recount the miracle of the draught of fishes. You don't have to have a seminary degree or specialized training to tell others what God has done in your life. Explain the changes in your life since being saved. It doesn't have to be eloquent or long-winded. It only needs to be from the heart.

Let's face it, none of us is worthy to be used of God. Nevertheless, He has enlisted each of us to perform great works for Him. Are we working? Are we obeying? There are multitudes of fish out in the deep. Let's go catch some!

DÉJÀ VU

Interestingly enough, there is another Biblical account that is so similar to this one that they're often confused. Same sea. Same crowd. Same results. Talk about déjà vu! (Have I said that already?)

Simon Peter saith unto them, I go a fishing. They say unto him, We also go with thee. They went forth, and entered into a ship immediately; and that night they caught nothing. But when the morning was now come, Jesus stood on the shore: but the disciples knew not that it was Jesus. Then Jesus saith unto them, Children, have ye any meat? They answered him, No. And he said unto them, Cast the net on the right side of the ship, and ye shall find. They cast therefore, and now they were not able to draw it for the multitude of fishes. Therefore that disciple whom Jesus loved saith unto Peter, It is the Lord. Now when Simon Peter heard that it was the Lord, he girt his fisher's coat unto him, (for he was naked,) and did cast himself into the sea. (John 21:3-7)

This passage takes place after Jesus' resurrection and after He had appeared to the disciples in His resurrected body on more than one occasion. In short, the disciples had received proof that everything Jesus had said was true. Yes, He had died. Yes, He had been buried. And yes, He was living again. You would think the disciples would have been thrilled. You would think they would be champing at the bit to get out and tell others what they now knew. But instead, they decided to turn to their old ways.

"I go a fishing" was not Peter's way of saying, "I think I'll take a day off and relax with some fishing." On the contrary, it was his way of saying, "I'm going back to fishing for fish. I've tried the fishing for men thing and look where that got us. Besides, I'm not worthy to be fishing for men. I denied Christ. I'm not worthy to tell others about Him. Nope, I'm only good enough for the fish." And in that moment of self-defeat, he turned from God's will. And you know what they say, "Misery loves company." That must be true because the remaining disciples declared, "Yea, we'll go with you." They might as well have said, "We quit too!"

Before we go any further, I want to back up and take a look at verse 2. I want you to get a good look at this rag-tag group of fishermen.

There were together Simon Peter, and Thomas called Didymus, and Nathanael of Cana in Galilee, and the sons of Zebedee, and two other of his disciples.

Okay, let's break this down. There's Peter, the denier. The one who stood up to Jesus and said, "Not me! I'll die for you" and then proceeded to deny Christ not once, but three times.

Then there's Thomas, the doubter (though, as I've already mentioned, that title could fit all the disciples).

The sons of Zebedee were James and John, the dividers. You remember James and John, right? They're the two that sent their mother to ask Jesus for special placement around the throne in Heaven. They desired to be elevated above the other disciples, and that kind of attitude led to division amongst the disciples, which is evidenced by their later argument over who would be greatest in Heaven.

And then there are two unnamed disciples who we'll call the drifters. We don't know who they are, and they probably prefer it that way. These unnamed disciples seem to just follow the crowd. If the main group stays, they'll stay. If the main group goes, they'll go. Like a feather, they drift wherever the winds blow them.

Is it any wonder this group failed to catch any fish? They weren't where they were supposed to be, and they weren't doing what they were supposed to do. And yet, we see that God still blessed them.

TAKE COMFORT

I don't know about you, but when I don't feel well physically, I am an emotional and spiritual mess. Who knew physical sickness could bring about such feelings of sorrow, loneliness, discouragement, and bitterness? And of course, those feelings would not be complete without their comforts.

Yes, chocolate cake calls to me and offers me solace. Sodas and sweets sing songs of peace and contentment. Processed foods promise me joy and delight. And the combination of all the above is surely the remedy that cures all ills. And so I've indulged in all they have to offer, and I'm sorry to say that they fell short of living up to their claims. I didn't receive solace, peace, contentment, or satisfaction. On the contrary, I received only guilt (and a lot of unnecessary calories). I'm guilty of allowing my emotions to turn my heart from the one true Source of comfort.

With that in mind, I see where Peter was coming from when he uttered, "I go a fishing." All hope seemed lost. Everything was in shambles. What seemed like a good thing had turned out bad. And I'm sure Peter was plagued daily with guilt over denying the Lord after his bold proclamations of standing strong. Yes, Peter could relate to feelings of sorrow, loneliness and discouragement. And so, in the midst of such feelings, Peter did the only thing he could think to do—he went back to his old ways. He had been a fisherman before. He would be a fisherman again. I think Peter sought comfort in something that came naturally to him, fishing. What a blessing that the Comforter had plans of His own.

Did you notice that John had to tell Peter it was the Lord who was on the shore and calling out to them? Peter was so distracted by his frustration and his "comforts" that he failed to recognize the Comforter, even when He was standing before him. But when he did realize who it was, something clicked. It was like Peter finally realized that only Jesus could comfort his hurting soul. And in Peter's mind, he couldn't reach the shore fast enough. He wasn't willing to wait on the boat. He threw himself into the water and swam with all his might. In desperation, he hurried to Jesus, and it was there he found his comfort.

How about you? Are you seeking comfort today from things that never fully satisfy? Are you turning to other people or things to bring you peace? Are you so distracted by the trials of life that you fail to recognize the answer to all your problems standing before you?

Look up, my friend.

That's Jesus standing there with outstretched arms.

He is the one true Source of comfort. Run to Him. Cry on His shoulder. Allow Him to heal your broken heart. And leave the bad habits in the boat, or better yet, toss them into the sea from whence they can never be recovered.

DINNER, ANYONE?

And the other disciples came in a little ship; (for they were not far from land, but as it were two hundred cubits,) dragging the net with fishes. As soon then as they were come to land, they saw a fire of coals there, and fish laid thereon, and bread. (John 21:8-9)

You simply cannot retell this story without taking a moment to notice what Jesus was doing. He was fixing dinner for the disciples. He was providing for the rag-tag group that had given up all hope. He was reminding them that there is nothing greater than grace. In His love and compassion, He was determined to feed both their bodies and souls. And if that weren't enough, he allowed them the opportunity to contribute.

Jesus saith unto them, Bring of the fish which ye have now caught. (John 21:10)

Jesus didn't need their fish. He had fish on the fire. He had cooked fish. He didn't need their offering. But just as He did with Lazarus, He allowed the disciples the opportunity to take part in a miracle. No, they didn't really have anything to do with the miraculous draught, but their catch played an important role in the miracle that is often overlooked.

THE OVERLOOKED MIRACLE

Simon Peter went up, and drew the net to land full of great fishes, an hundred and fifty and three: and for all there were so many, yet was not the net broken. (John 21:11)

In verse 6, the Bible tells us that the disciples were not able to draw up the net because it was so full and heavy. To further illustrate the point, it goes on to tell us that they had to drag the net alongside the boat. Seven strong men could not lift the nets out of the water. Pretty clear picture, huh?

But when Jesus directed them to bring in the fish they had caught, the Bible says, *Simon Peter went up, and drew the net to land full of great fishes*. Simon Peter, one man. Not all the disciples. Not a few of the disciples. Not Jesus, the God-man. No, just Peter. At that moment, Peter could do what the seven of them could not do earlier. When was the last time you saw one man carry a net containing 153 fish? How is that even possible? I'm so glad you asked!

First of all, when Peter was out fishing, he was acting in his own strength. He had given up on the Lord. His return to his job as a fisherman was basically his saying, "Well, that fisher of men thing didn't work out like I planned, so I'll just go back to what I know." But that wasn't where God wanted Him. I think Jesus intended to show Peter (and us) that when we act in our own strength, our efforts are in vain.

Second, I think Jesus was reminding us that He will give strength when strength is needed. In the midst of the direst circumstances, Jesus can give strength to move mountains. If God calls us to do something, He will always equip us with what we need to accomplish the task. No matter how small or great the task may seem, His strength is always sufficient.

But the question that weighs foremost in my mind is this: How did Peter know he could do it? When Jesus said to get the net, why didn't Peter ask for help? Wouldn't that have been the logical thing to do? "Hey, John, can you give me a hand here?" But he didn't.

He didn't seek help.

He didn't complain about the task.

He didn't leave the task for someone else.

He didn't hesitate.

According to the passage, he didn't even say anything. Now, that's a first for Peter, huh?

But how did he know? Could it be that all those lessons Jesus had been teaching for the past three and a half years finally sank in? Maybe that last miracle was the proverbial straw that broke the camel's back. Perhaps Peter had finally figured out that Jesus was the Almighty God. All I know is that Jesus commanded for it to be done, and Peter did it.

Just yesterday, I sang a song in church entitled, "I'll Do the Miracle."[1]

The message of the song is simple, yet profound. Our job is not to try to figure things out or to make sense of God's commands. Our job is to do what He's called us to do and then trust Him to do the rest. That's it! We're not responsible for the results. That's not our place. Our place is to trust and obey. As the song states, we are to do what's possible and leave the miracles to God. He's never failed, and He never will. No matter how strange

His instructions may seem, follow on. He has a task for you to do, and He'll provide whatever you need to see it through.

And that's no fish tale!

Section Six: Miracles Missing in Action

HE'S STILL WORKING MIRACLES

Chapter Eleven:

MASSIVE MISTAKE OR MYSTERIOUS MERCY?

And it came to pass, when Jesus had made an end of commanding his twelve disciples, he departed thence to teach and to preach in their cities. Now when John had heard in the prison the works of Christ, he sent two of his disciples, And said unto him, Art thou he that should come, or do we look for another? Jesus answered and said unto them, Go and shew John again those things which ye do hear and see: The blind receive their sight, and the lame walk, the lepers are cleansed, and the deaf hear, the dead are raised up, and the poor have the gospel preached to them. And blessed is he, whosoever shall not be offended in me. And as they departed, Jesus began to say unto the multitudes concerning John, What went ye out into the wilderness to see? A reed shaken with the wind? But what went ye out for to see? A man clothed in soft raiment? behold, they that wear soft clothing are in kings' houses. But what went ye out for to see? A prophet? yea, I say unto you, and more than a prophet. For this is he, of whom it is written, Behold, I send my messenger before thy face, which shall prepare thy way before thee. Verily I say unto you, Among them that are born of women there hath not risen a greater than John the Baptist: notwithstanding he that is least in the kingdom of heaven is greater than he. - Matthew 11:1-11

It's been one of those weeks. You know the kind. The ones where you simply want to crawl into bed and issue the command, "Wake me up when this week's over." Yes, that has been the week I've had. On Tuesday, we lost power at our house due to severe thunderstorms. Have you ever tried to type a book, submit online articles, or enter new blog posts when the power's out? It doesn't work. My entire life came to a standstill, and I didn't know what to do with myself. I contemplated doing a little housework, but good sense overruled that decision, so I did what I could and prayed for the power to be restored before I lost my sanity.

On Wednesday, I had a nerve-wracking doctor's appointment that I had not been looking forward to. For the most part, things went well, but I was given some less-than-pleasant news and charged a boatload of money for the opportunity to be poked, prodded, and interviewed with twenty questions. As if my nerves weren't frayed enough by the time I left the doctor's office, I received a phone call from my sister who informed me that they had put their cat down that morning. Talking to her about the difficulty of saying goodbye to lifelong members of the family brought back a fresh wave of painful memories of having to put down our dog, Tessa, a few years back.

Overall, I felt saddened and completely out of sorts. By the time I got home, I had decided that I wasn't going to try to do any "real work" for the rest of the afternoon, even though the power had been restored. I gave myself permission to take it easy until church that evening, that is, after I made a couple of phone calls. You see, I had ordered a couple of trial products and had been trying to cancel the services before I was billed for more products at an extremely ridiculous rate. By that point in time, my emails had gone unanswered, and my attempts to cancel via the website had been unsuccessful. Despite my hatred of talking on the phone, I decided it was the best course of action. The first call went well and took only a few moments. The second call, however, had me on hold for quite a while. When I finally got someone on the phone, I explained why I was calling and then had to go through the run-around of expounding on my reasons for canceling. Just as the operator was pulling up my account information, my phone decided to shut itself off. My first thought was that the battery had died, but no, when I booted the phone back up, I saw that there was plenty of battery left. It had just decided to go off, which meant I had to call and go through that entire process all over again. I was less than happy!

I had high hopes for Thursday since it was the fourth of July and Jason was off work during the day. We had planned a pleasant hike with the dogs and some much-needed rest time for the evening. Unfortunately, we woke to rain showers and scattered thunderstorms. Determined to carry out our plans, we packed our bags and headed toward the hiking trail, praying all the way that the weather would clear. It didn't. Even with our rain gear, we were quite wet by the time we returned to our vehicle. Still, we reasoned it was nothing that a nice change of clothes wouldn't cure. And for a while, all was well. . . until about an hour before Jason was supposed to leave for work, and he came down with a terrible sinus headache. Unable to shake it, he decided to move his cleaning job until Friday night, which made for a very long day on Friday, but the alternative was to go in his present condition, and neither of us liked that plan.

For a little icing on the cake Thursday, I found out that an article I had written for a company would have to be deleted due to some error with guidelines on the company's end. No payment. No publication. Just the knowledge that I had wasted an hour and a half of my time on an article that I'll never see again. Before I could gather any more information about the entire ordeal, my internet went down.

As of right now, it's still down!

We called the cable company this morning, and based on the information we gave them, they decided it was probably an issue with our equipment, possibly resulting from all the severe weather we've had of late. They informed us that the soonest a technician could get to us would be Saturday afternoon.

No good. We have a family gathering.

Sunday? Still no good. We leave early for church and don't return home until after church Sunday evening.

That left Monday morning, which means I missed my article deadlines, I can't post to my blog, and I can't do any social networking. I can't even watch my favorite show on Netflix. I feel cut off from the world. Sure, I could pack up my stuff and go down to the local sandwich shop to use their WiFi, but one of the greatest things about working from home is that I can do it from HOME. The whole process just loses something when I actually have to get out of my pajamas, fix my hair, put on some makeup, pack up my laptop, and drive somewhere. Where's the fun in that? Thankfully, my

208

word processing program works just fine without the internet, so I figure this chapter should keep me busy for a while. My external hard drive, on the other hand, is also giving me trouble. While I was trying to access a file from it this morning, it notified me that the entire drive was corrupted or unreadable. That's bad, bad news. There's a ton of information on that hard drive, and now I don't know if I'll ever be able to access it.

I wish I could tell you that I was making some of this up or simply exaggerating the facts, but I'm afraid not. You have just read a summary of my week, and maybe now you understand why I'm tempted to crawl under the covers and stay there until things look a little brighter and run a little smoother. To steal a phrase from Charlie Brown, good grief! Enough is enough. Still, I'm trying to remind myself that as bad as things seem, someone somewhere is having a far worse week than I am and I still have much for which to be thankful.

TALK ABOUT A BAD WEEK!

If ever there was someone who experienced a bad week, it would have to be John the Baptist. Good old John. The camel-hair wearing, locust-eating, boldly-proclaiming cousin of Christ Himself. Yes, he certainly stood out in a crowd, but not for the reasons you might think. It wasn't his appearance that made people whisper. It wasn't his relationship with Jesus that caused the crowds to flock to his meetings. It wasn't even his record of never having lost someone to drowning during the baptism. No, it wasn't any of those things. It was his zeal. It was his brutal honesty. It was his boldness to stand up and state the truth, no matter whose feelings were hurt in the process. But most of all, it was his humility.

John could have made much of himself. He had baptized hundreds if not thousands. He had his own band of disciples. He was related to the Messiah. He was the forerunner of Christ. The one prophesied to clear the way for the One who would rule and reign for all eternity. Though a little strange when it came to his choice of clothing and culinary delights, he was respected by the people and even by the royalty of the day, so much so that some of them even wondered if he was the Messiah. He had accomplished much. He had every reason to be proud. Yet he wasn't. On the contrary, he was always quick to turn the attention away from himself and toward Christ. He assured the crowds that he was not the Messiah, only the one to bear witness of the Messiah. So deep was his humility that he went on to state that he wasn't even worthy to fasten Christ's sandals.

I could go on and give you many more examples of John's humble nature, but I don't want you to take my word for it. Instead, why don't you look at what Jesus had to say about his cousin?

Verily I say unto you, Among them that are born of women there hath not risen a greater than John the Baptist. (Matthew 11:11a)

Did you catch that? None greater. Not David. Not Solomon. Not Abraham or Noah. Of all those who had been born, Christ considered none greater than John the Baptist. If that's not high praise, I don't know what is.

But I think it's also what makes the rest of John's story so difficult to understand.

John had all the right credentials. He was doing all the right things. He had dedicated his entire life to pointing souls to Christ and baptizing in the name of Christ. He was a man on a mission. A relative and a friend. He had so much to live for.

Yet John had a date with death.

John ticked off the wrong person. When he stood before Herod and told the king, in no uncertain terms, that he was committing adultery by marrying his brother's wife, John didn't mince words. He said what he meant and meant what he said. He proclaimed the truth, and that proclamation landed him in jail. And there he sat, day after day, waiting for his release or, at the very least, a visit from his cousin, Jesus. Surely, when word got to Christ, He would hurry to John's aid. And if not, perhaps God would send an angel like He did for Peter or an earthquake like He did for Paul. Yes, John was hopeful. Deliverance would come. But after a while, John's optimism wore thin, and the preacher found himself facing some of Satan's deadliest darts.

ASSAILED BY DOUBT

We know from the Scriptures that some of John's disciples visited with him on at least one occasion, so it's safe to assume they had other opportunities to talk with the prisoner. During these visits, the disciples, no doubt, told John all about Jesus' continuing ministry—the people that were being healed, those who were following Christ, and the many other miracles that were being accomplished. All good news, right? In a sense, yes, but to John, the news had to have been somewhat distressing. I imagine one such conversation taking place like this:

"Yes, John," says Disciple 1, "Jesus is growing in popularity every day. The people are following him everywhere."

"That's good," John says as he looks up from the floor. "Does He know where I am? Did you tell Him what happened with Herod? Is He aware that I'm facing a death sentence?"

The two disciples look at one another then lower their gazes.

"Um," stutters Disciple 2, "Yes, He knows. We told Him everything. We pleaded with Him to come to your rescue. We really did."

John's expression becomes more hopeful. "And what did He say? What did He do?"

Again, Disciple 1 lowers his gaze. "He moved on in the opposite direction. We don't understand it, John. He's carrying on with business as usual. It's like He doesn't even care about what's happened to you. Why doesn't He come?"

No doubt, John was wondering the exact same thing. And secure on the wings of that question was another question. A question John never imagined he would ask or have a need to ask.

"Go back to Jesus and ask Him if He's the One we've been waiting for or if we should look for someone else?"

Arrows away!

The Bible tells us that Satan has fiery darts that he shoots our way to throw us off track and to shift our focus from the truth of God's Word. A single dart, in and of itself, is a danger to be sure, but unfortunately, they seldom travel alone. Once we've been hit by one, it's only a matter of time before we're hit with another and then another.

John was in a prime place for just such an attack. He was tired and weary. He was confused and afraid. And worst of all, he felt forsaken, abandoned by the very One he had been promoting.

Coming from a loving family, I didn't really understand much about abandonment until my first trip to the Humane Society. Yes, some of the animals were strays, and others were there for other reasons, but the majority of the cages were inhabited by lonely animals that had been abandoned. Turned away from their homes and families. Taken to an unfamiliar place with strange people. Forced to make the cut for "cute and cuddly" or face the consequences of the unlovable. In some pounds, that penalty was to remain in the cage for extremely long periods of time, but for others, the penalty was death. If an animal couldn't convince some loving soul to adopt it, they were sentenced to be put down. While I understand the reasoning behind this cruel-sounding act, I still cringe every time I think about it.

Perhaps that's why I've never owned a pet from a pet store even though I've had a cat or dog all my life. No, most of my animals have been from the Humane Society. I cherish the thought of rescuing some poor creature from a life of imprisonment or a sentence of execution. I long to do what I can to make the unlovable feel loved once again.

Those feelings may also be the motivation behind my desire to choose from the adult animals rather than the puppies and kittens. Don't get me wrong. I love puppies and kittens. Who doesn't? But that's the point. Who doesn't? Everyone wants to pick from the puppies and kittens, but so few even visit the adult cats and dogs. Most of the time, since they're in a separate section (usually in the back), the adult animals don't even get a chance to try to win the heart of some caring soul. But with me, they all have the opportunity to be adopted. I'll give each one a fair chance, although I must admit that once one has captured my heart, I find it difficult to do more than glance at the others. Such was the case when we adopted our shepherd mix, Mitchell.

From the moment I saw him, my heart broke. Never in my life have I seen such a sad face. Standing quietly at the cage door, he watched as Jason and I made our way up and down the aisle of the cramped shelter. As we neared him, he pressed his face again the door. He never barked, cried, or whimpered. He only looked at us, but that look spoke volumes. It said, "I'm afraid and alone. I don't want to stay here any longer. Please take me home with you. I just want to love and be loved. Please don't forsake me. I've already suffered that. Don't make me suffer anymore."

With tears in my eyes, I reached out to pet his head. He nuzzled my hand and breathed a heavy sigh of contentment. And my mind was made up. I wanted to take him home with me then and there, but Jason reminded me of my commitment to give every dog a chance and insisted that I look at the rest of the animals. I did look, but to be honest, I had no intention of choosing a different dog. I had found the dog I wanted. I had found the dog who needed me as much as I needed him. And, in the end, after we had looked them all over, I stated my decision. Jason only smiled and commented that he knew Mitchell was the dog we would end up with as soon as he had seen him. "I knew you couldn't resist that face," he said.

He was right. I couldn't

Yet, somehow God could. I'm sure John's expression was just as pitiful as Mitchell's. I'm certain his somber eyes contained the same misery and betrayed his feelings of abandonment. God knew how John felt. He knew what was happening. He understood the turmoil reeling inside this righteous man, yet He did nothing (or so it would seem). No miraculous rescue. No voice from Heaven. Nothing!

Why is God often silent? When we need to hear from Him the most, why does He choose to withhold His voice? I'm afraid I don't know the answer to that, but what I do know is that during those times when God is silent, Satan's whispers ring through loud and clear. Just ask John. I'm sure he heard a few things.

"God doesn't care about you. You've spent your entire life paving the way for a fraud. He's not the Messiah. Can't be. He's not the One you were sent to prepare the way for. All your work has been in vain. You've got nothing left. Here you sit all alone in this filthy prison cell, and the One you put your trust in can't even be bothered to come visit you. He probably couldn't help you if He tried. You're done, John. You might as well look forward to your beheading because you don't have anything worth living for anyway." Fire Dart #1 – Deception

We must beware of the way the devil intermixes truth and falsehood. Yes, John had put his trust in Christ. Yes, John had devoted his entire life to the cause of Christ. But the truth stopped there. Unfortunately, when we're down and discouraged, it's easy to forget. We forget the truth of God's Word. We forget the miracles we've seen. John did. As he sat there listening to Satan spin his web of deception, John forgot the prophecies he had read and quoted. He forgot about the dove and the voice that spoke, "This is my beloved Son in whom I am well pleased" at Jesus' baptism. In that prison of isolation, he forgot everything he knew.

"Maybe he's right," John reasoned. "Maybe I've had things all wrong. After all, I thought the Messiah was going to come and establish His kingdom. Jesus certainly hasn't done that. He hasn't exactly done things the way I thought he would. I mean, sure He's done miracles and all, but still, there's something that's not quite right. Maybe it's the people He hangs out with. Some of them are of questionable character. Is it logical to assume that the King of Kings would hang out with thieves and harlots? Hardly. But more than anything, I just can't believe that the Messiah would leave me here to die. After all, I'm doing His work. I'm pointing people to Him. The prophecies say that the Messiah will set the captives free. I'm a captive, but have I been freed? Hmm, something's just not right." Fire Dart #2 – Doubt

Jesus had said, *And ye shall know the truth, and the truth shall make you free.*[1]

John knew the truth. But more than that, John knew the TRUTH. Jesus is the way, the truth, and the life. John knew that. He was related to the Truth. He baptized the Truth. He introduced the people to the Truth. Yes, John knew the Truth, but there seemed to be some kind of hold up on the latter part of that verse. John wasn't set free. And when one verse doesn't work out the way we expect it to, we begin to doubt the rest. If only we'd understand that it's not the verse or promise that's flawed but rather our interpretations of it. John knew better, but the enemy fire was growing heavier by the minute. Fire Dart #3 – Discouragement. Fire Dart #4 – Discontentment. Fire Dart #5 – Defeat.

John was desperate. He needed to know what was going on. He needed an answer. So he sent out his disciples and waited anxiously for the response.

Although it took every ounce of what was left of his assaulted spirit, John the Baptist acknowledged his faith's crisis by verbally extending a weary hand of doubt in hopes of being able to grasp onto something, something that could pull him to a fragment of belief.[2]

WHAT KIND OF ANSWER IS THAT?

As ordered, the disciples went to Jesus and put forth John's question. Jesus' answer was brief and quite vague. The disciples, no doubt, were hoping for a straightforward answer like, "Go tell John that I am the One" or "Tell John not to be afraid. The Great I Am is in control." Short and sweet. That's the kind of answers we like, isn't it? Ask a straightforward question; get a straightforward answer. But Jesus' answer was a quotation from the book of Isaiah. Actually, it was part of a quotation from the book of Isaiah. He conveniently left out the portion that speaks of the captives being set free. Had He forgotten that part? Absolutely not. Did He misquote Scripture? Hardly, He's the author. Whatever His reasoning behind leaving out that portion, I have to believe it was in John's best interest. Perhaps that portion of the prophecy would have only added to John's confusion, like rubbing salt in a wound.

So what did Jesus' answer mean? Why didn't He just answer "yes" or "no"? Could it be that He knows we often learn the lesson better when we figure it out for ourselves after being reminded of His Word? Maybe I have that theory because I taught kindergarten and lower elementary for nine years. When dealing with certain students, it was often tempting to tell them the answer rather than to show them how to find the answer for themselves. Telling them the answer was easy. It was quicker. It was less painful for the student and teacher both. Everybody's happy, right?

Maybe. . . until the student faced another similar problem and was still unprepared to find a solution because I had cheated him out of a lesson for the sake of ease and comfort. I had to remind myself over and over again that I was not doing them any favors by telling them the answers or doing the work for them. I showed them how to find the solutions and helped them when I could, but I insisted that they come to their own conclusions. They were responsible for the work, and I was responsible for teaching them how to complete that work.

It seemed harsh, especially to some of the parents who didn't understand or share my reasoning behind teaching the child to think for himself and to learn the skills required to solve problems on his own. But, it never failed, before the end of the year, both parents and students were thanking me for not taking the easy road. In the end, they realized the benefit of being equipped to come to the proper conclusions.

Jesus' directions and responses are not always black and white, but He's given us His Word to help us come to the correct conclusions. No matter what situation we may face, the answer can be found in God's Word. Sometimes, we just need to be reminded. God has to draw our attention away from our circumstances and our doubts and force us to remember what we know. And if we'll let the truth of His Word sink in, we'll discover the answers we've been seeking.

John doubted Jesus' identity as the Messiah, so Jesus reminded him of what the Bible said about the One for whom John was supposed to prepare the way. "The blind will see, the deaf will hear, the lame will walk. The dead shall be raised. John, you've heard about my ministry. What is that I've been doing?"

What had He been doing? Well, let's see. Healing the blind, the deaf, and the lame. Raising the dead and cleansing the lepers.

I believe, in His own special way, Jesus was telling John, "Yes, it's me, John, and everything's going according to plan."

John was trying to plan for tomorrow, but Jesus was planning for eternity.

John was troubled about the now, but Jesus was concerned about the everlasting.

John was seeking the assurance of another day, but Jesus was fulfilling the requirement for eternal life.

John was looking at the present, but Jesus was looking to the future.

There was a much bigger plan in place than what John realized. In his doubt and confusion, he'd forgotten that his tomorrow was uncertain, but, because of Jesus, his forever was sure. Jesus took care of that.

WHAT DO YOU SAY TO THAT, JOHN?

It is a mystery to me that the Bible does not tell us John's response to Jesus' answer. Did he get it? Did he understand what Jesus meant? Did his outlook change? Did he die a happy man? For whatever reason, God didn't see fit to let us in on the end of John's story. We know that he died a cruel and horrible death. We know that he was beheaded for doing nothing more than standing up for the truth. But concerning his response to Jesus' statement, we're left to guess.

I'd like to believe that John got the message loud and clear. In my mind's eye, I envision his disciples shuffling up to the cell door, neither wanting to be the bearer of bad news.

"Well," John coaxes, "what did He say?"

Disciple #1 swallows hard. "He said to tell you that the blind will see, the deaf will hear, the lame will walk, the dead will rise again, and the lepers will be cleansed."

For a moment, John is perplexed. The words sound familiar. If only he could remember, and then it clicks. A smirk appears on his lips as he begins to nod his head. "So He is the One. I knew it. I just knew it!"

I would hope that the same smirk was on his face when his head was presented on the silver platter. In a way, it's a morbid thought, but it's also a symbol that he died at peace. His heart and mind were clear. He was no longer troubled by doubt and discouragement.

I wish we knew, but I can tell you this much— John is certainly at peace now, and all his questions have been answered.

THE DEBATE OVER JOHN'S DOUBT

There are many that theorize that John's question to Jesus was not a sign of doubt, but rather a lesson of trust for the sake of his disciples. These scholars state that John sent his disciples to question Jesus for their assurance, not his own. I can certainly see the possibility of such a case, but what I don't agree with is their reasoning behind the theory. Basically, they deny John's doubt because they claim that he couldn't have possibly doubted Christ after all that he had seen and heard.

Granted, John was the greatest man born of women (besides Jesus, of course), but he was a man, nonetheless. Even the righteous can fall. No man is exempt from Satan's temptations and deadly attacks. Yes, John had seen a lot, but so had the disciples, and they doubted Christ until after His resurrection. To say that John was incapable of doubting is placing him on a pedestal on which he doesn't belong. In a sense, they are attributing him with sinless perfection, and that's the kind of worship that John was always redirecting to Christ where it belonged.

As to John's motives, again, we can only guess, but one thing we can know for certain—John was never forsaken. He may have felt that way. It may have seemed that way. But God was there the entire time. He never left John's side, and He'll never leave yours. Jesus made certain of that. As He hung on Calvary's tree, He was abandoned. His disciples had run away. The angels were forbidden to interfere. Even His Father had to turn away because He couldn't bear to look at the sin that covered our Savior and Lord. For a time God was forsaken of God, and in the pain and terror of that separation, Jesus cried out, "My God, My God, why have you forsaken me?"

And though God was silent, His answer quickly became evident. Jesus was forsaken so that we never would be. With His blood, He purchased for us a place of belonging that can never be taken away. We'll never be cast aside. We'll never be alone. And while we may not get the miracle for which we were praying, God still cares. He hears our cries. He honors our questions. He even understands our doubts. But He also loves us enough to look beyond our present circumstances and expectations to our future needs and accomplishments. And when we consider that, we realize that our miracles are not missing but rather that our expectations are misplaced. John expected deliverance, and in a sense, that's exactly what he got. It just wasn't the way he had in mind.

What are you expecting today? Whatever it is, don't give up on it. Don't let your doubt and confusion steal away the truths that you know and cling to. Hope in God's Word. Trust in His promises. And leave the results up to Him. You'll get your miracle. . .

Just remember it may come forth much differently than you were expecting.

But that's okay. Who doesn't love a good mystery?

Chapter Twelve:

WHEN GOD SAYS "NO"

It is not expedient for me doubtless to glory. I will come to visions and revelations of the Lord. I knew a man in Christ above fourteen years ago, (whether in the body, I cannot tell; or whether out of the body, I cannot tell: God knoweth;) such an one caught up to the third heaven. And I knew such a man, (whether in the body, or out of the body, I cannot tell: God knoweth;) How that he was caught up into paradise, and heard unspeakable words, which it is not lawful for a man to utter. Of such an one will I glory: yet of myself I will not glory, but in mine infirmities. For though I would desire to glory, I shall not be a fool; for I will say the truth: but now I forbear, lest any man should think of me above that which he seeth me to be, or that he heareth of me. And lest I should be exalted above measure through the abundance of the revelations, there was given to me a thorn in the flesh, the messenger of Satan to buffet me, lest I should be exalted above measure. For this thing I besought the Lord thrice, that it might depart from me. And he said unto me, My grace is sufficient for thee: for my strength is made perfect in weakness. Most gladly therefore will I rather glory in my infirmities, that the power of Christ may rest upon me. Therefore I take pleasure in infirmities, in reproaches, in necessities, in persecutions, in distresses for Christ's sake: for when I am weak, then am I strong. - II Corinthians 12:1-10

For years, scholars have debated about the thorn that Paul speaks about in the above passage. The possibilities and assumptions are vast and varied. One of the most common beliefs is that Paul suffered from poor eyesight, which is certainly plausible. We know that He was blinded on the road to Damascus, so it is possible that his eyesight was never fully restored or that the temporary blinding left lasting effects that were set in motion over time. In Galatians 6:11, Paul writes, *Ye see how large a letter I have written unto you with mine own hand.* There is no way to determine whether Paul was speaking of the length of the letter he had written or if he was referring to the size of the print he was using because of poor eyesight. Many believe it is the latter.

WHAT A PAIN IN THE NECK!

Based on some observations of Paul's writings, other scholars believe that Paul could have possibly suffered from a major illness or disease such as seizures or epilepsy. Such illnesses would have numerous symptoms and would have certainly hindered Paul's work for Christ. I can attest first-hand as to how illness and injury can throw a monkey wrench in even the best intentions.

In the eleventh grade, I was injured during an out-of-state basketball game. A cheerleader at the time, I was doing my best to encourage school spirit and cheer on the players of our team. At one point during the game, one of the opposing players chased the ball, ran off the court and into me. Unfortunately, our cheerleading squad was standing in front of a waist-high wall that separated the court from the concession area. When the player stumbled into me, we both went over the wall, but I went over backward. From the moment my back hit the wall, I knew something was wrong, but at the time, my embarrassment seemed more pronounced than the pain. I sat out the rest of the game, and by the time we loaded onto the bus to head home, I was nearly in tears from the pain.

I waddled around the next couple of days, the pain ever-present. By the third day, I stumbled to my parents' bedroom to tell them I didn't feel up to going to school. By the time I reached their doorway, I passed out from the pain. Needless to say, we were at the hospital in short order. Many hours and x-rays later, the doctors informed us that one of my lower vertebrae was no longer sitting horizontally but rather on a diagonal. This shift was causing severe pinching of the nerves between that vertebra and the vertebra above and below it. The options were two: (1) Have surgery to place a pin in my spine to hold the vertebra in place. Unfortunately, this particular surgery came with only a fifty percent success rate and held the possibility of complete paralysis from my waist down. (2) Live with it. I opted for choice number two.

I wish I could say that my spine miraculously fixed itself, but I'm afraid that's not the case. Instead, I've spent more than half my life with a painful injury that has become a breeding ground for severe arthritis and hindered me in more ways than I can explain. Additionally, arthritis and bursitis have flared up in my wrists, knees, and shoulders. Whether these other instances are results of my injury, I do not know. For the

227

most part, I lead a normal, and even active life. In fact, most of my friends are not even aware of the injury and the constant pain (although, they probably are now). But there are times when I simply can't hide it. The pain is too great. And during these times, I, like Paul, plead with the Lord to remove the thorn.

Please understand that I'm not telling you this for pity or sympathy. I merely want you to understand that I've been there. I've been at the place where I wondered what God was thinking when He allowed such an accident. I've been at the place where I couldn't do the things I wanted to do because of physical hindrances. I've been at the place where my very work for God was set back because of something He allowed to happen in my past, something that He could have prevented. Yes, if Paul's thorn was illness or injury, I can relate, as I'm sure many of you can as well.

THINGS THAT GO BUMP IN THE NIGHT

It's also possible that Paul's thorn in the flesh, the "messenger of Satan" as he calls is, was a literal messenger of Satan—an evil spirit. We know they are out there, all around us. We hear their voices as they call out to us to do the wrong things, go the wrong places, and think the wrong thoughts. They persuade and justify, connive and complain, argue and question. Hour after hour, day after day, they are after us, doing everything in their power to lead us astray.

Don't you know that Satan wanted to hinder Paul's work? Look at the multitudes he was leading to Christ. Paul was thwarting Satan's plans, and Satan wasn't happy about it. It wouldn't surprise me in the least if he sent some of his top demons to harass and tempt Paul. Perhaps it was just general harassment or perhaps the demons knew all the right buttons to push. In Hebrews 12, the Bible speaks of the sin which so easily besets us. Is it possible the demons knew what sin Paul struggled with the most and constantly dangled that sin in front of his eyes like the forbidden fruit it was? While Satan is not omniscient like God, he is wise and picks up on our words and actions and is then able to use that knowledge to plan our demise. He may have done the same with Paul.

For whatever reason, Paul doesn't specify what his thorn was. It may have been too personal for him to mention, or he may have felt that such detail was not necessary. What we do know, however, is that the Bible was written under the inspiration of God, and I'd like to think that maybe God left the specifics of Paul's thorn ambiguous so that we could insert our own thorn in the blank. You know, there was given to me a _____. Illness. Injury. Divorce. Death in the family. Bankruptcy. Disabled child. You fill in the blank with whatever it is you're facing or have faced, and suddenly, Paul's story becomes your story. His pleas become your pleas. And God's answer? Well, we'll get to that soon.

LIONS AND TIGERS AND THORNS, O MY!

However different your thorns may be from mine, all thorns have a few things in common. They irritate. They annoy. They tear at our most vulnerable spots. And when left untended, they can fester into something much worse than the thorn itself.

Jason and I do a lot of hiking. I've found that it does wonders for my ailments and is just as therapeutic for my soul. There's something about strolling through the woods and trekking up a mountain that brings peace to a troubled heart and restless mind. Hiking gives us time to talk, but it also gives us time to think. We've come to cherish the times we can pack the bags, get away and hide from the world in the haven of the wilderness.

As much as we love hiking, however, summer in the upstate of South Carolina does not present the ideal hiking environment. For starters, it's hot! But beyond that, there are snakes (both poisonous and non-poisonous), bugs of every shape and size, spider webs by the hundreds and briers. Lots and lots of briers. They tear at my clothes. They embed themselves in my socks. They grab at my hair and skin. We've actually been on some trails where it seemed the briers actually reached out and latched onto my flesh. It's not uncommon to see one or both of us with huge scratches on our arms and legs from simply trying to walk a trail.

Briers. Thorns. Same thing as far as I'm concerned. Those pesky little things can make even the most beautiful hike unbearable. I get frustrated with having to stop every few steps to untangle some part of me from their treacherous grip. I become agitated at their constant clawing and scraping. They block the path. They hinder the view. They stall my progress. And they fester, not only in my skin but also in my attitude. Nobody likes thorns!

So, it's no surprise that Paul asked God repeatedly to remove the thorn from him. I can certainly understand Paul's point of view. He was living for the Lord. He was doing the right things. He was winning others to Christ. Wouldn't his ministry be more effective if he weren't hindered by a thorn? To our mere mortal minds, the whole thing just doesn't make sense. From our way of thinking, we would surmise that God would remove the stumbling blocks, not allow them, right? But God doesn't think as we think, does He? No, His thoughts are above our thoughts. So far above, in fact, that we can't even comprehend the hows and whys of it all. All we can do is trust that God will do for us what He did for Paul. He gave him what he needed instead of what he wanted. God said, "no" to Paul's request so that He could say "yes" to something even greater for the apostle.

From the human standpoint, though, it's never easy to discover that our requests have been denied. It's frustrating and sometimes even heartbreaking. Such was the case for Mark and Lisa Dibler.

RESURRECTION GROUND

Happily married with two young daughters, Mark and Lisa were living their lives for the glory of the Lord. Not only were they faithful church attendees, but they were also part of a singing group that traveled the country to spread the good news of Christ. Humble. Honest. Hardworking. These are just a few ways to describe the devoted servants who put God first in their lives. Nevertheless, a great trial was awaiting them, and

231

it was through this trial that their true loyalties would be tested.

In 1991, Mark and Lisa noticed that their oldest daughter, Marie, was sleeping later and later into the morning with each passing day. Since the couple worked nights cleaning a restaurant and took their two girls with them, they naturally assumed she was simply catching up. Before long, however, she also began spitting up regularly and complaining of headaches. These new symptoms concerned Mark and Lisa, but it was the events of one memorable Sunday morning that caused them to take the next step in discovering what was going on.

During the regular morning church service, Marie came from the back room, basket in hand, to take up the offering. She nearly ran into the communion table, not as if she had stumbled, but as if she hadn't even seen that it was there. Mark noted this, but before he could mention it to Lisa, more trouble arrived. Marie, tears flowing, ran from her Sunday School class and into Lisa's arms. Her Sunday School teacher, Mrs. Roper, informed the troubled parents that Marie had climbed into her lap during Sunday School and had repeatedly complained that her head hurt. The couple took her to the hospital where they checked her vitals and set up an appointment with the family doctor.

The following days involved countless doctor and hospital visits as well as more headaches and vomiting from Marie. On Thursday, the doctors ran a cat scan. From the moment the couple saw the doctor's face, they knew the news was not good. Three-year-old Marie had a brain tumor. Mark and Lisa were devastated, but their hope was somewhat renewed when they spoke to a specialist who made it seem as if things were not as bad as they seemed. He had a plan and set about scheduling further tests and treatments. Little did he know that God had a plan as well.

A little more than a week later, the specialist performed the surgery to remove the bulk of the tumor. The family, along with numerous friends, sat breathlessly in the waiting room. Prayers abounded, and tears flowed, but above all, God's presence filled the room. The surgery was scheduled to last ten hours. The nurses updated the family every two hours to keep them aware of the progress, but at the eighth hour, no update came. The family waited until the ninth hour, and when no one came to them, they went and inquired about Marie.

Within moments, a doctor escorted them into an unoccupied room. He began by explaining that the tumor was much larger than any of them had anticipated and that it possessed tentacles that were wrapped around every part of Marie's brain. There was also a major blood vessel running through the middle of the tumor, making it impossible to extract the entire thing. The doctors tried to cut away what they could, but during the surgery, Marie's heart had stopped beating. The physicians were able to revive her, but at that point in time, there was no way to know whether she would have brain damage or any other side effects. There was nothing for Mark and Lisa to do but wait and pray.

That night, Marie's brain continued to swell. By six o'clock the next morning, they were rushing her back to surgery to help relieve the swelling. The doctors removed part of her right temporal lobe and informed the parents that if Marie survived, she would have to be completely retrained, like an infant. At this point, that was fine with Mark and Lisa, just as long as they could have their little girl. They were willing to do whatever was necessary. Their only concern was Marie's survival.

For the next few days, Marie's condition worsened. Her brain continued to swell. Her heart rate slowed. Her organs began to shut down one by one. And after the second surgery, all brain activity ceased. She was living entirely on machines. The grieved couple faced a heart-wrenching decision. In their pain, they found a quiet place to pray and pleaded with God for direction. On the one hand, they couldn't believe that God would want them to lose their precious child, but on the other hand, they understood that God knew best and was in control of all things. In the middle of their prayer, a verse came to Mark's mind as if it were being whispered in his ear: *Suffer the little children to come unto me, and forbid them not: for of such is the kingdom of God.*[1]

At that moment, Mark knew they had their answer. A few hours later, Marie Dibler passed from this life.

Mark's uncle, Dr. Russell Rice, was asked to speak at Marie's funeral, and during that mournful time, he spoke words that have encouraged thousands since then. Dr. Rice commented that in the world's view, they were standing at a grave, but for the Christian, the grave is resurrection ground. As Mark and Lisa walked home that day (they lived only moments from the cemetery), the Lord gave Mark the words to a song. A song born of grief and tragedy, but one that has touched the lives of hundreds, if not thousands of people. The song is entitled, "Resurrection Ground."[2]

We gathered together to say our goodbyes
To our sweet little girl,
Oh, how our hearts ached inside.
Then we went to the place
Where they lowered her body down.
Some call it a grave;
I call it resurrection ground.

Resurrection ground; no more graves allowed,
We'll meet her in the air; no more parting there.
With Jesus we'll be for all eternity.
This is not the end; it's resurrection ground.

We come here often
To see where she lay,
It doesn't seem so long ago,
She ran around and played.
How sweet it would be
If we were standing 'round
When this whole place
Turns to resurrection ground.

Resurrection ground; no more graves allowed,
We'll meet her in the air; no more parting there.
With Jesus we'll be for all eternity.
This is not the end; it's resurrection ground.

Since the composition of this song, several groups have recorded it, a multitude of choirs have sung it, and it has been used (as both a song and a poem) at funerals all around the world. It has brought comfort to many who were grieved over the loss of a loved one. It has also been a beacon of hope to those who didn't know where to turn in their grief. Yes, this one song has made a world of difference. Could that be why God allowed Marie to die? Was that His plan all along? I don't think we'll ever know the answer to that on this side of Heaven, but I can tell you what Mark and Lisa have to say about it. "To know that song was being sung and that it was helping others was a healing process for me," Lisa confided. "Even though it was a bitter experience, I think I'm a better person because of it," Mark added.

Though the situation was heart-breaking, Mark and Lisa made a decision that they would not get mad at God. They determined that their loss would not pull them away from the church or their service to the Lord. While the following weeks, months and even years were difficult, the couple clung to God's promises and strove to live in His will, knowing that while Marie's passing was a shock to them, it was certainly not a shock to God.

Naturally, there have been times that Mark and Lisa have questioned why God didn't give them the miracle for which they so fervently prayed. Fortunately, because they continued to walk with the Lord despite their suffering, they have now grown in their faith enough to realize that God did grant them a miracle. It simply wasn't the miracle they were expecting. Paul learned the same lesson when God answered him, *My grace is sufficient for thee: for my strength is made perfect in weakness.* God told Paul that He would give him the grace and strength to recognize and accept the miracles that God gave, even when they weren't the miracles for which he had asked. God gives us the grace and strength to do the same.

If Mark and Lisa had gotten the miracle they desired, the song "Resurrection Ground" would have never been written. How many miracles have resulted from that one song alone? You see, God loved the Diblers too much to give them what they wanted. He, instead, gave them what they needed, and that miracle has served as the seed for a multitude of other miracles. And how about Paul? If he had gotten the miracle he desired, would he have been the same Paul that we see in the Bible? Would he have had the same zeal? The same faith? Would he have been as close to the Lord?

Sometimes it takes a storm before we'll look for the Savior to come walking on the water. And sometimes that storm takes the form of an absent or delayed miracle. I am not qualified to tell you why God chooses to answer some prayers in the affirmative while choosing to not answer others in the same way. He's God, and He doesn't have to explain Himself to us. The truth of the matter is this: God doesn't work the same way in every life. He is a personal Savior, and He has a personal plan for each of us. We're talking about the God who doesn't make any two snowflakes alike nor any two fingerprints. What makes us think He'll work in each life in the exact same way? Sometimes He speaks to the storm, but other times He walks on the sea. Sometimes He touches the sick while other times He commands them to obey. Sometimes He frees the prisoner on this side of Heaven, but sometimes He frees them on the other. It's all in accordance with His personal plan for each individual.

He knows our names.

He knows our talents.

He knows our temperaments.

And He knows our future.

As for your miracle, I agree with Candise Farmer. *The miracle—having the power of God resting upon us—is the most precious, valuable commodity in all of our earthly existence.*[3] Even if you never receive the miracle for which you so earnestly prayed, you will receive something greater. To each of us, God promises His grace and His power. And if we're honest, we'll admit that *that's* all we really need.

PRINCIPLES OF PRAYER

Despite what many scholars and preachers may tell you, I don't feel there is only one right way to pray. In fact, if you'll read through the Bible, you'll see many styles of prayer. There is no perfect time of day. There are no magical words. There is no specific order or time frame. When it comes to prayer, if you'll allow the Spirit to guide you, He'll let you know all the specifics.

That being said, there are a few principles of prayer that the Bible speaks of on numerous occasions. We see the principles modeled by David, Paul, and even Jesus. By applying these principles to your prayer life, you are bound to find yourself drawing closer to God and becoming more prayer-focused in all areas of your life.

◆ **Pray with persistence.**

Paul didn't say that He asked God once to remove the thorn. He kept asking. Obviously, once God told him "no," I believe Paul stopped asking, but until God gives you a clear answer, don't stop asking. I have a friend who prayed for his father-in-law's salvation every single day for fourteen years. Without fail, he prayed, never growing discouraged. A few years ago, his prayers were finally answered, and his father-in-law accepted Christ as Savior. Whatever you're praying about, don't give up. It pays to pray.

◆ **Pray in earnest.**

It is important to show God that we're serious about our prayers. In the hustle and bustle of today's world, it's so tempting to mutter out a prayer for this and that without really even paying attention to what we're asking for. When Jesus prayed in the Garden of Gethsemane, his prayer was so intense that He sweat blood. He was earnest in His request, and through His prayer, He was showing God that He meant business. We should do the same. The Bible tells us to approach His throne boldly. That's not to say we should be arrogant, but rather that we should not hold back in telling God what's on our hearts and minds.

◆ **Pray specifically.**

If we want specific answers, it's about time we started making specific requests. I recall a time in my life when finances were very tight (as they usually are), and I made a request of the Lord. Half-joking, I prayed that I would receive a check for $300 in the mail. Believe it or not, that very same day, there was a check for $300 in my mailbox. Unfortunately, it was a check from an automobile retailer that could only be used in the purchase of a new vehicle. God did answer my prayer; I just wasn't specific enough in my request. Yes, God knows what we need, but He still longs for us to ask. Get specific. Are you praying about a thorn? If so, then mention that exact thorn. It's easy to generalize. "Lord, bless the church." "Lord, heal our infirmities." "God, please help me." It's high time we say what we mean and mean what we say!

◆ Accept God's answer when it comes.

As I already mentioned, if God does not give you a clear answer, by all means, you should keep praying. However, if God tells you "no" or "wait," don't continue to make the same request in hopes that He'll change His mind. When God gives you a final answer, accept it along with the grace and strength He offers for you to carry on. Don't pout. Don't whine. Don't get mad at God. These behaviors only create a spirit of bitterness. Accept that God has a reason and trust in Jeremiah 29:11 which says, *For I know the thoughts that I think toward you, saith the LORD, thoughts of peace, and not of evil, to give you an expected end.* If God says "no," He must have a greater "yes" around the corner. Don't give up. Don't give in. There's a miracle in the making!

240

NOTES

CHAPTER ONE: MORE MOUTHS THAN MONEY

1. See I Corinthians 14:40.
2. See I Kings 17:16.
3. See Ephesians 3:20.

CHAPTER TWO: THE GREAT ESCAPE

1. Oswald Chambers, *My Utmost for His Highest*, (Grand Rapids, Michigan: Discovery House Publishers, 1992), n. pag.
2. Nick Vujicic, *Unstoppable: The Incredible Power of Faith in Action*, (Colorado Springs, Colorado: Waterbrook Press, 2012), 3.
3. Nick Vujicic, *Unstoppable: The Incredible Power of Faith in Action*, (Colorado Springs, Colorado: Waterbrook Press, 2012), 10.
4. Charles Stanley, *How to Listen to God*, (Nashville, Tennessee: Thomas Nelson, 1985), 100.
5. Warren Wiersbe, *Meet Yourself in the Psalms*, (Wheaton, Illinois: Victor Books, 1986), 47.

CHAPTER THREE: MARY HAD A LITTLE LAMB

1. Joseph Smith and Ronnie Booth, "In His Time," See http://christiansongoftheday.blogspot.com/2012/10/in-his-time.html
2. Karen Kingsbury, *A Treasury of Christmas Miracles: True Stories of God's Presence Today*, (New York, New York: Warner Books, 2001), n. pag.
3. See Luke 2:19.
4. Debbie Morris, *The Blessed Woman: Learning About Grace from the Women of the Bible*, (Colorado Springs,

Colorado: Waterbrook Press, 2013), n.pag.

CHAPTER FOUR: JAILHOUSE ROCK

1. Warren Wiersbe, *Meet Yourself in the Psalms*, (Wheaton, Illinois: Victor Books, 1986), 93.
2. Jerry Bridges, *A Study Guide on the Best-Selling Book Trusting God Even When Life Hurts*, (Colorado Springs, Colorado: NavPress Books, 1989), 12.
3. See Acts 16:31.
4. Ron Mehl, *Surprise Endings: Ten Good Things About Bad Things*, (Sisters, Oregon: Multnomah Press, 1993), 136.

CHAPTER FIVE: A TALE OF TWO MIRACLES

1. Sheila Walsh, *The Shelter of God's Promises*, Nashville, Tennessee: Thomas Nelson, 2011), 85.

CHAPTER SIX: HELLO, MY NAME IS _____

1. Henry Cloud and John Townsend, *What to Do When You Don't Know What to Do*, (Nashville, Tennessee: Thomas Nelson, 2009), 86-87
2. Warren Wiersbe, *Meet Yourself in the Psalms*, (Wheaton, Illinois: Victor Books, 1986), 73.
3. See Psalm 107: 8,15,21,31.

CHAPTER SEVEN: WHATCHU TALKIN' 'BOUT, JESUS?

1. David Jeremiah, *A Bend in the Road: Experiencing God When Your World Caves In*, (Nashville, Tennessee: Thomas Nelson, 2000), 45.
2. Max Lucado, *Life's Lessons with Max Lucado: But Joy Comes in the Morning*, (Nashville, Tennessee: W Publishing Group, 2000), 41.
3. Warren Wiersbe, *Meet Yourself in the Psalms*, (Wheaton, Illinois: Victor Books, 1986), 73.

4. Joanna Weaver, *Lazarus Awakening: Finding Your Place in the Heart of God*, (Colorado Springs, Colorado: Waterbrook Press, 2011), 65.
5. See I Thessalonians 4:13-14.
6. Henry Cloud and John Townsend, *What to Do When You Don't Know What to Do*, (Nashville, Tennessee: Thomas Nelson, 2009*), 69.*
7. See Psalm 56:8.
8. Marshall Hall and Benji Gaither, "When I Cry," See http://christiansongoftheday.blogspot.com/2009/05/when-i-cry.html.
9. Harold B. Sightler, John, (Greenville, South Carolina: Tabernacle Baptist Church, 1986), 117.
10. See Philippians 4:6.

CHAPTER EIGHT: TALES FROM THE CRYPT

1. See Romans 8:38-39.

CHAPTER NINE: FOOTPRINTS ON THE WATER

1. See Hebrews 13:5 and Deuteronomy 31:6.
2. Max Lucado, *A Gentle Thunder*, (Nashville, Tennessee: W Publishing Group, 1995), 28.
3. Max Lucado, *In the Eye of the Storm*, (Nashville, Tennessee: Word Publishing, 1991), 202.
4. See LynnMosher.com: http://lynnmosher.com/take-the-bread-with-you-even-if-its-just-the-crumbs-2/
5. Ron Mehl, *What God Whispers in the Night*, (Sisters, Oregon: Multnomah Publishers, 2000), 61.

CHAPTER TEN: GOD FILLS EMPTY NETS

1. Rodney Griffin, "I'll Do the Miracle," See http://christiansongoftheday.blogspot.com/2012/09/ill-do-miracle.html.

CHAPTER ELEVEN: MASSIVE MISTAKE OR MYSTERIOUS MERCY?

1. See John 8:32.
2. Candise Farmer, *Green Pastures of a Barren Land: Finding Contentment in Life's Desolate Seasons*, (Carrollton, Georgia: Free Church Press, 2012), 127.

CHAPTER TWELVE: WHEN GOD SAYS "NO"

1. See Mark 10:14.
2. Mark Dibler, "Resurrection Ground," See http://www.abishaimusic.com/.
3. Candise Farmer, *Green Pastures of a Barren Land: Finding Contentment in Life's Desolate Seasons*, (Carrollton, Georgia: Free Church Press, 2012), 149.

ABOUT THE AUTHOR:

Dana Rongione is the author of several Christian books, including the highly-praised **Giggles and Grace** devotional series for women. A dedicated wife and doggie "mom," Dana lives in Greenville, SC, where she spends her days writing and reaching out to the hurting and discouraged. Connect with her on her website, DanaRongione.com, and be sure to sign up for her daily devotions.

HE'S STILL WORKING MIRACLES

BOOKS BY DANA RONGIONE:

Devotional/Christian Living:

There's a Verse for That

'Paws'itively Divine: Devotions for Dog Lovers

The Deadly Darts of the Devil

What Happened To Prince Charming?: Understanding What To Do When You No Longer Know the Man You're Married To

Giggles and Grace Series:

> Random Ramblings of a Raving Redhead
> Daily Discussions of a Doubting Disciple
> Lilting Laments of a Looney Lass
> Mindful Musings of a Moody Motivator

Other Titles for Adults:

Improve Your Health Naturally

Creating a World of Your Own: Your Guide to Writing Fiction

The Delaware Detectives Middle-Grade Mystery Series:

Book #1 – The Delaware Detectives: A Middle-Grade Mystery

Book #2 – Through Many Dangers

Book #3 – My Fears Relieved

Books for Young Children:

Through the Eyes of a Child

God Can Use My Differences

Audio:

Moodswing Mania – a Bible study through select Psalms (6 CD's)

The Names of God – a 6-CD Bible study exploring some of the most powerful names of God

Miracles of the Old Testament, Part 1 – a Bible study with a unique look at miracles in the Old Testament (4 CD's)

There's a Verse for That – Scripture with a soft music background, perfect for meditation or memorization

MAY I ASK A FAVOR?

Thank you for purchasing and reading my book! I really appreciate all of your feedback, and I love hearing what you have to say.

I need your input to make the next version (and all future books) better.

Please leave a helpful REVIEW of this book on Amazon, Goodreads, or your favorite reading site.

Thank you so much!

HE'S STILL WORKING MIRACLES

HE'S STILL WORKING MIRACLES